WHAT ◆ IS VALUE

THE OPEN COURT
LIBRARY OF PHILOSOPHY

SERIES EDITOR
Eugene Freeman
SAN JOSE STATE COLLEGE

What Is Value?

An Introduction
to
AXIOLOGY

Second Edition

By

RISIERI FRONDIZI

Visiting Professor of Philosophy, Southern Illinois University.
Former Visiting Professor of Philosophy, Universities of
Pennsylvania, Yale, Texas, and University of California at
Los Angeles.

OPEN COURT PUBLISHING COMPANY
Established 1887
La Salle, Illinois
1971

Library of Congress Catalog Card Number: 70-128196

WHAT IS VALUE?

SECOND EDITION

Printed in the United States of America

Contents

PREFACE TO THE SECOND EDITION

This is an introduction to value theory. The author has done his best to reduce its complex problems to clear issues. In the first chapter there is an elementary presentation of the principal characteristics of value. In the second, the reader will find the basic issues, which could be reduced to the question: do we desire things because they are good or are they good because we desire them? In the third chapter the main subjectivistic doctrines are discussed, and in the fourth Max Scheler's objectivism is presented and analyzed. In the last chapter the reader will find an attempt to overcome the antithesis between subjectivism and objectivism.

This second edition is based on the fourth Spanish edition. A selective basic bibliography has been added to each chapter, and many changes, not only in style, have been introduced. The main change is the interpretation of value as a Gestalt quality. A Gestalt depends on but cannot be reduced to the empirical qualities. With this interpretation the author hopes to take care of G. E. Moore's concern about the relation of *good* to the natural qualities.

There is no need to point out the increasing importance
of value theory. Not only ethics, esthetics and philosophy
of education, but also sociology, cultural anthropology
and many other disciplines show a growing interest in
value theory. An expression of this increasing interest is
the publication of *The Journal of Value Inquiry* devoted
entirely to this discipline.

The author is responsible both for the contents of the
book and its translation into English, and wishes to express
his thanks to everyone who helped to improve the present
edition.

Risieri Frondizi

Department of Philosophy
Southern Illinois University
July 9, 1970

PREFACE TO THE FIRST EDITION

The interest in value theory which continues to mount at a rate equalled only by the increase and diversification of the bibliography involved would seem to call for an overall inquiry into its present status as a whole. In general, research in this field has been one-sided in nature, and the efforts made have been motivated to a greater extent by the desire to prove a point than by the wish to explain a complex reality. Hence, the frequent impression that very little progress has been made, and that the problem is still at the point of departure.

If one should wish to reduce the constellation of axiological problems to a single issue, there is no doubt that the one involving the nature of value should be selected. The two opposing theories—subjectivism and objectivism—which arose originally, are today still very much in evidence. Furthermore, they even find their way into the minds of those who are not conscious of the complex philosophical problems involved. Are things valuable because we value them or do we value them because they are valuable?

As has happened on many other occasions in the history of philosophy, the origin of the impasse is due to the way in which the problem is posed, rather than in the proposed solutions. Hence, the need for a complete reformulation of the question.

In Chapter V the errors of both doctrines are pointed out, and after summarizing the positive aspects of each, an attempt is made to overcome the impasse by way of a new approach to the problem.

The first two chapters constitute an elementary and schematic introduction to value theory itself, addressed to the reader who is not familiar with the complex problems involved in contemporary axiology. In order to present a coherent outline to those who are not too well acquainted with value theory, certain rather thorny problems have had to be considered solved for the moment; however, they are restated in the final chapters. It should not be forgotten that the book endeavors, at one and the same time, to be an introduction to axiology, a summary of its basic problems, and an attempt to indicate the path which leads to the solution of a barren *status quo.*

The bibliography has been reduced to an indispensable minimum for the purpose of helping the reader rather than making a display of information. The more than ample lists of titles in existence are capable of satisfying his curiosity if he wishes to penetrate further into the jungle of contemporary bibliography in axiology.

I am grateful to the Open Court Publishing Company for the interest shown in making possible the publication of this work.

Risieri Frondizi

University of Buenos Aires
February 1962

TRANSLATOR'S NOTE TO THE FIRST EDITION

Future Historians may well refer to the present century as the age of intensification of conflict. This is a period in which technological advance has aggravated beyond measure and calculation the consequences of culture crisis and ideological clash. The rise of new nations, the self-assertiveness of hitherto "suppressed" peoples, the never-ending challenges to the *status quo*, and the resultant re-evaluation and readjustment required to meet them, all bring into sharp focus the underlying premises upon which individual and group behavior patterns as well as entire governmental systems are based. The re-examination of some of these assumptions by troubled consciences leads inevitably to the problem of what sort of values we live by. Thus, the battle of ideologies is essentially related to a conflict between value systems.

Is this ideological warfare and the failure to resolve differences the result of an axiological relativism which makes of philosophy a mere matter of opinion? Or is there an objective character in values which can be arrived at, once semantic roadblocks are eliminated, or at least minimized? In answer to this question, one more analysis of value theory, added to those already published, seems more than welcome, especially when it comes to the English-speaking public from the pen of a foremost representative of philosophy "south of the border."

If differences in value theory are basic to ideological clash, then it can be said that Dr. Risieri Frondizi is himself a living example as well as a victim of the conflict in values. Because of his opposition to the Perón regime, he was dismissed from his post at the university. Self-imposed exile was the result, an exile which, happily, was to end once the Peron government was overthrown.

Dr. Frondizi's effective and comprehensive analysis of value theory, presented for the first time to American readers, is the result of many years of distinguished scholarship. An outstanding philosopher, not only in his native Argentina, but in all of Latin America as well, he has taught in the leading universities of the continent, e.g., Venezuela, Mexico, Puerto Rico, Colombia, as well as in three universities of Argentina. He is no stranger to the United States, having pursued part of his studies for the doctorate at Harvard University under Whitehead, Köhler and Perry. He has been visiting professor at Pennsylvania, Yale, Columbia, and has lectured at Harvard, Michigan, Texas, .Wesleyan, Swarthmore and Bryn Mawr. Some of these fruitful endeavors were made possible by the Perón dictatorship, so that Argentina's loss was, temporarily at least, our gain. However, Dr. Frondizi did not restrict his activities to the Western Hemisphere. He has also lectured at the Universities of Rome, Brussels, Turin, Milan and Amsterdam. He has been President of the University of Buenos Aires (1957-62) and professor of ethics (1956-66). He is a member of various international philosophical organizations, including the Phenomenological Society, the American Metaphysical Society, and the Inter-American Federation of Philosophy. He was the President of the Union of Latin American Universities and a member of the

Administrative Board of the International Association of Universities.

Dr. Frondizi is a prolific writer and has contributed to numerous philosophic journals in both Europe and America. Among his books, *El punto de partida del filosofar* and *Substancia y función en el problema del yo* have called forth highly favorable reactions and stimulating comments on the part of American critics, such as Patrick Romanell, Charles Hartshorne, Alfred Stern, Nicola Abbagnano, and the late Edgar S. Brightman. The latter book is available in an English translation under the title *The Nature of the Self*, published by Yale University Press.

It is in connection with the published works of Latin American thinkers and philosophers that one must note a curious, yet most regrettable fact insofar as United States-Latin American cultural relations are concerned. In the past century or so, Latin American intellectuals seem to have been very much aware of our thinkers here in the United States, and what these represent. This is much truer than its converse. Very few thinkers in this country are familiar with intellectual currents, not to mention philosophic thought, of Latin America. True, not all Latin Americans have admired us; some have criticized us, often harshly so. But the fact remains: our cultural contributions find their echo in the consciousness of Latin America; theirs do not, to the extent that they should, vis-à-vis our intellectual awareness. This condition is simply illustrative of the inadequacy of communication of *ideas* between the two Americas—a condition which cries out for correction.

No one would take issue with the statement that the surest road to the essence of a culture is via a knowledge of the intellectual fermentation that goes on among the people who create that culture. What is there in that culture that is distinctive? What are some of the facets that are different from ours? Or, if there are similarities, what are they? Latin American philosophy, for example, in contrast to philosophic tendencies in the United States, seems to concern itself with problems usually found in the areas designated as "man and society," "humanism," "values," and "culture." Philosophy in this country, by contrast, places a greater emphasis on such themes as scientific knowledge, logical positivism and symbolic logic. If this is so, then it becomes obvious that the need for these two American philosophies to complement each other was never more apparent. This interchange of ideas, this cross-fertilization, will, it is hoped, result in mutual enrichment for all concerned. It is with this hope that this modest translation of the work of a distinguished Latin American philosopher is offered to the English-speaking public.

I wish to express my appreciation to Dr. Frondizi for making possible an extended correspondence which proved most cordial and fruitful. His generous co-operation helped surmount those linguistic hurdles which might have impeded the exact interpretation of a phrase or concept. For all possible errors in translation, I assume full responsibility.

Solomon Lipp

Boston University
1962

What Is Value?

1. The World of Values

Value theory is very popular today, but it did not exist a century ago. While metaphysics and ethics flourished in Ancient Greece, and theory of knowledge started in the 17th century, value theory, also called axiology, was not formulated until the end of the 19th century.

Man was concerned about values from the very beginning, and philosophical theories about particular types of values have since Plato been the subject of many profound pages. But it is only since the last century that justice, goodness, beauty and other particular values were studied not only in their specific nature, but also as members of a new genus called *value*. This was a real discovery and it consisted basically in distinguishing *being* from *value*. The ancients, as well as the moderns, subsumed value under being without realizing it, and measured both with the same yardstick. The early attempts at axiology were directed without exception to separate value from facts. Today, the study of isolated values acquires new meaning when one notes not only the subtle thread which binds them together, but also the ray of light which all research casts upon the nature of value. Hence, ethics as well as esthetics, of ancient philosophical lineage, have in recent years taken a long step forward because of the study of value as such.

The discovery of a new area cannot be underrated. If philosophy tends by its very nature to give an explanation of the totality of what exists, anything unearthed which broadens our vision will be a true philosophic discovery. The discovery of an area hitherto unexplored is as important as a new explanation of the world, if not more so; for we cannot be satisfied with an interpretation that has failed to encompass an entire area, because it did not consider all of its categories. Every discovery focuses attention on itself, to the temporary neglect of what is already known. The initial reaction consists in forcefully attempting to accommodate things to the modality of the recent arrival. One tries to see the totality of the world through the crack opened up by the new discovery. This explains the enormous proliferation of works on axiology and the attempt to reduce the whole of philosophy to value theory.

What has this new area been added to? What regions had already been explored when values were discovered? Since its beginnings, philosophy endeavored to present an all-embracing vision of the totality of the world. But from the very beginning, too, it confused totality with one of its aspects. Western philosophy began 26 centuries ago with a concern for the nature of the external world. When the Ionians, in the 6th century B.C., asked themselves what was the principle or *arché* of reality, they understood reality to mean nature, the external world. Hence, for their answer they selected material substances, such as water, *apeiron* or air. The outer world, then, is the first subject of philosophic research, and "things," in the customary sense of the term, the first form of reality. But a people possessed of the rational capacity of the Greeks (it has been extravagantly claimed more than once that the Greeks "discovered" reason) such a people could not resign itself to the contemplation of the physical world. It soon became aware that besides this world, there exists another of equal or greater significance, an ideal world, so to speak. It is the world of essences, concepts, relations, i.e., of that which today goes by the name of ideal objects. The Pythagoreans, Socrates and Plato are the discoverers of this world of essences.

Psychic phenomena were later added to physical reality and ideal objects. Besides stones, animals, rivers and mountains, and numbers, concepts and relations, there

exist my own experiences, my grief and my joy, my hope
and my concern, my perceptions and my memory. This
reality is undeniable; nevertheless, it was so close to man
that it took him a long time before he noticed it. Just as
the eye, according to Locke's analogy, sees external
objects and only years afterward discovers itself, the mind
at first turns toward the outer realm, and, once it has
matured, it looks back upon itself.

When a new area is discovered, two contrary
movements are generally produced. One, to which we have
already referred, and which is led by the greatest
enthusiasts of the discovery, tries to see everything in
terms of what has just been discovered, and endeavors to
see the old reality in terms of the new. In opposition to
this movement, there appears another which attempts to
reduce the new to the old. While some maintain that all
philosophy is but axiology, others insist that values do not
constitute a novelty, that a new name has merely been
discovered to designate old modes of being.

What could values be reduced to, according to this
latter conception? We have thus far indicated three great
sectors of reality: things, essences, and psychic
phenomena. At the outset, the attempt was made to
reduce values to experiences. Value is equivalent to that
which pleases us, said some; it is identified with what is
desired, added others; it is the object of our interest,
insisted a third group. Pleasure, desire, interest, are
experiences; value, for these authors, is reduced to mere
personal experiences.

In direct opposition to this psychological interpretation
of value, there arose a theory which soon acquired great
meaning and prestige, and which came to the conclusion,
similar to that of Nicolai Hartmann, that values are
essences, Platonic ideas. The error committed by some
philosophers in thus merging values with essences is due in
part to the confusion, between unreality—a peculiar sign of

value, and ideality which characterizes essences. The supposed intemporality of value lent considerable support to the doctrine which tries to include values in the same category as ideal objects.

If, indeed, no one has tried to reduce values to the status of things, there is no doubt that the former have been confused with the material objects which embodied them. The confusion originated in the very real fact that values do not exist by themselves, but depend, rather, upon some value carrier or support, which is generally of a corporal substance. Thus, beauty, for example, does not exist by itself, floating as it were in mid-air, but is, instead, embodied in some physical object: a piece of cloth, marble or bronze. The need for a carrier in which it is embodied lends a peculiar character to value, condemns it to a "parasitical" existence, but such peculiarity cannot justify the confusion between value and the object in which value is embodied. In order to avoid confusion in the future, it would henceforth be well to distinguish between values and value objects.[1] Value objects are valuable *things*, that is, both the thing and the value embodied in it. Thus, a piece of marble is a mere thing; the hand of the sculptor adds beauty to it by "taking away all that is unnecessary," according to the ironic suggestion of a sculptor, and the marble thing is transformed into a statue, into a beautiful thing. The statue continues to preserve all the characteristics of ordinary marble—its weight, its chemical composition, its hardness, etc.; nevertheless, something has been added which has changed it into a statue. What has been added to it is an esthetic value. Values are, therefore, neither things nor experiences, nor essences; they are values.

1. Called *Güter* in German and *bienes* in Spanish.

2. Value as a Gestalt Quality

Well then, what are values?

It has been pointed out that values do not exist for themselves, at least in this world; they need something in which to be embodied or a carrier.[2] Therefore, they appear to us as mere qualities of these value carriers: beauty *of* a picture, elegance *of* a garment, utility *of* a tool. If we observe the picture, the garment, or the tool, we shall see that the value quality is different from the other qualities.

In the objects mentioned there are some qualities which seem essential to the very existence of the object: extension, shape, impenetrability and weight, for example. None of these objects could exist if any of these qualities were missing. On the other hand, they are qualities which valuable objects share with other objects and which these objects possessed before any value was attached to them. The existence of the object depends on these qualities, but value does not bestow or add existence, since the stone fully existed before being engraved, before it was transformed into something beautiful. Basic qualities without which objects could not exist are called "primary qualities." Besides these, there are "secondary qualities" or sensible qualities, such as color, taste, smell, etc., which can be distinguished from the "primary," due to their greater or lesser degree of subjectivity. Whether color is a subjective impression or whether it is located in the object, it is evident that there can be no iron or cloth or marble which does not possess color. The color belongs to the reality of the object, to its very being. On the other hand, elegance, utility or beauty are not necessarily part of the object, since things which do not contain these values can

---

2. *Träger* in German and *depositario* in Spanish.

exist.

Samuel Alexander has called values "tertiary qualities," to distinguish them from the other two categories of qualities. The designation is found wanting, because values are not a third kind of the same type of quality, but rather, a new kind. It would be more appropriate to assert that values are "unreal qualities," although not ideal, as they do not add reality to objects, but only add value. Regardless of the label we use, it is certain that values are not things nor elements of things, but properties, qualities, *sui generis*, which certain objects that we may call valuable objects possess.

Since qualities cannot exist by themselves, values belong to that class of objects which Husserl calls "not independent," that is, they do not possess substantiveness. This fact, apparently very simple, is a fundamental characteristic of values. Certain objectivist theories have made many extravagant claims, because they forget that value is a quality, an adjective, and by treating it as a noun have fallen into senseless speculation and hence found it impossible to discover its peculiar character. Present-day philosophy has cured itself of the traditional tendency to substantivize all the elements of reality. On the contrary: what stands out today are verbs, adjectives and even adverbs. Behind many traditional nouns there is an implicit adjective. One should not be misled by language. Language assimilates forms of thinking which are prevalent, and a new idea cannot remain a prisoner of language; it requires linguistic habits which should adapt themselves better to new forms of thinking.

Because they are qualities, values are parasitic beings which cannot live without being supported by real objects, and lead a fragile existence. While primary qualities cannot be eliminated from objects, a few hammer blows will suffice to put an end to the utility of an instrument or the beauty of a statue. Before getting embodied in value objects they are but mere possibilities, potentialities haunting real existence.

One should not confuse values with essences, relations or concepts. The difference can best be seen if one compares beauty, which is a value, with the idea of beauty, which is a concept. Beauty may be grasped primarily through emotions, while the idea of beauty is apprehended intellectually. A work dealing with esthetics does not arouse emotions in us, since it is made up of concepts and propositions which are intellectual in their nature and meaning. This is not so in the case of a poem, where the metaphor which the poet employs expresses an emotion and is meant to arouse an emotion in the reader. It would be foolish, for instance, to reject Keats' famous lines: "A thing of beauty is a joy for ever" because it is not true.

It has been pointed out that values are merely potentials, unreal qualities. They are unreal in the sense that they do not constitute part of the object in which they are embodied, as extension, shape and other primary and secondary qualities do. You may take value out of a physical object without destroying it; you cannot do the same with extension, for instance. In another sense, values are real while they are embodied in real objects called value objects such as statues, poems, cars, houses, paintings.

The unreality of values should be interpreted as a Gestalt quality. A Gestalt is more than the aggregate of its constituent parts, and is a new quality which arises from a unique configuration of these parts, which are not homogenous. At the same time, a Gestalt should not be confused with a concept, since it has empirical, individual existence. A symphony orchestra is a good illustration of a Gestalt, but a poem, a painting, a cathedral or our own bodies are also *Gestalts.*[3]

If one interprets the so-called unreality of value as a Gestalt quality, one can understand the apparently contradictory fact that values depend on, but cannot be reduced to, the empirical qualities from which they spring.

3. Polarity and Hierarchy

A basic characteristic of values is polarity. Whereas things are what they are, values present themselves unfolded as it were in a positive and negative aspect. Thus, good and bad, beautiful and ugly, just and unjust, etc. It should not be thought that disvalue or negative value implies the mere lack of positive value; negative values exist by themselves, "positively," so to speak, and not because of the absence of the corresponding value. We find ugly objects around us, and not merely objects which lack beauty. The same is true of the other negative values.

It has often been pointed out that polarity implies a break with indifference. In the presence of objects of the physical world, we can be indifferent. On the other hand, the moment a value attaches itself to an object, such indifference is broken and we like it or dislike it, accept it or reject it, seek it or avoid it. We are not neutral when confronted with a work of art or a dishonest act. No one is indifferent as he listens to a symphony, reads a poem or looks at a painting.

Besides the fact that values are positive or negative, we find that they have a ranking; they are better or worse. This is both true of values and value objects. No two

3. For a more specific analysis of the notion of *Gestalt* and of values as Gestalt qualities, see Chapter V, Section 5.

poems or symphonies are on the same level; one is better than the other, though it is very difficult sometimes to tell which it is. In the same way, the "beauty" in the painting of Van Gogh seems to be superior to a pleasant ice cream. There seems to be a hierarchy in the nature of values and value objects.

Hierarchy should not be confused with a classification. Classification does not necessarily imply order of importance. One may divide men into fat and skinny, tall and short, single and married, without necessarily implying that one group is better than another. Values, on the other hand, are given in their order of importance or according to a ranking. Hierarchy is revealed in preference: upon being confronted with two values, a person will usually prefer the one he thinks is higher, although at times he may "choose" the inferior one due to circumstantial reasons like price, distance or any other advantage.

Of course, it is simpler to point out that a hierarchical order exists than to indicate concretely what that order is. True there have been axiologists who have proposed *a* table of values, and who have claimed that this was *the* table. Subsequent criticism has shown the weakness of such tables and of the criteria which were used to build them up. A specific instance is Max Scheler, presented in Chapter IV. Though it was considered to be established once and forever, yet it vanished in Scheler's lifetime.

The existence of some ranking among values is a permanent stimulus to creative action and moral elevation. The creative and lofty sense of life is based fundamentally on the drive for a positive value, as opposed to the negative, of a superior value as opposed to the inferior.

Individual man, as well as communities and specific cultural groups, guide themselves according to a standard. It is certain that such standards are not fixed; they fluctuate and are not always coherent. Yet, it cannot be denied that our behavior toward our fellow man, our judgments concerning his conduct and our esthetic preferences are adjusted to some kind of a set of values. To submit to critical examination these systems of values, which in some obscure fashion influence our conduct and our preferences, is the indispensable task of every enlightened individual. Nevertheless, he will be unable to determine critically a table of values—let us set aside the possibility of dogmatically positing a hierarchical order—without first examining the validity of the criteria to be used and the nature of value itself. These are the questions we shall discuss in the following chapter.

4. Bibliography

CHRISTOFF, D. J.; CURIEL, L.; EWING, A. C.; FRONDIZI, R.; HARTMAN, R. S.; and von RINTELEN, F. J. *Symposium sobre Valor en Genere y Valores Específicos.* México, D. F.: Univ. Nac. Autónoma de México, 1963.

EWING, A. C. *The Definition of Good.* New York: Macmillan, 1947.

HALL, E. W. *Our Knowledge of Fact and Value.* Chapel Hill: The University of North Carolina Press, 1961. See Part II.

_____. *What is Value? An Essay on Philosophical Analysis.* London: Routledge & Kegan Paul, 1952.

KÖHLER, Wolfgang. *The Place of Value in a World of Facts.* New York: Liveright Publishing Corp., 1938. New edition. Mentor Book, 1966. See Chaps. II and III.

HARTMAN, Robert S. *The Structure of Value.* Carbondale: Southern Illinois University Press, 1967. Arcturus Books Edition, 1969.

_____. *El conocimiento del bien. Fundamentos de la axiología científica:* México, D. F.: Fondo de Cultura Económica, 1959.

LAVELLE, Louis. *Traité des Valeurs.* 2 vols. Paris: Presses Universitaires de France, 1951-1955.

LEPLEY, Ray (ed.). *Value: A Cooperative Inquiry.* New York: Columbia University Press, 1949.

_____. *The Language of Value.* New York: Columbia University Press, 1957.

PARKER, De Witt H. *Human Values.* New York: Harper and Bros., 1931.

_____. *The Philosophy of Value.* Ann Arbor: University of Michigan Press, 1957.

RESCHER, Nicholas. *Introduction to Value Theory.*
        Englewood Cliffs, N. J.: Prentice-Hall, 1969.

For a good bibliography up to 1958, see Ethel M.
Albert and Clyde Kluckhohn. *A Selected Bibliography on
Values, Ethics and Esthetics,* 1920-1958. Glencoe, Illinois:
The Free Press, 1959.

A general but good survey of value theory in the first
half of this century in Robert S. Hartman, "General
Theory of Value," in *Philosophy in the Mid-Century: A
Survey.* Edited by R. Klibansky. Firenze: La Nuova Italia
Editrice, 1958. Vol. III, pp. 3-41.

Since 1968 there is a journal devoted entirely to
axiology: *The Journal of Value Inquiry.* Akron, Ohio:
University of Akron Press.

Basic
Problems
In
Axiology

1. Value Problems in Daily Life

Fundamental value problems are not only a concern of philosophers; they are also present in our daily life. There is not a discussion or disagreement about a person's behavior, a woman's elegance, or the enjoyment of a meal, that does not have as its basis a question of values. The most complicated axiological problems are debated daily in the street, in parliament, and in the most modest homes, although with an attitude and in a language which can hardly be called philosophical. Nevertheless, the discussions generally reveal the two extreme positions of axiology. When two people disagree whether a meal or a drink is pleasant, or not, each fails to change the other's opinion, one of them usually ends the discussion by saying that he likes it, and no one can convince him otherwise. If it is a discussion between educated people, then someone may recall the Latin adage: *de gustibus non est disputandum.*

This proverb can put an end to an argument, either of the ordinary or more sophisticated variety, but it does not solve the basic problem which underlies such discussion. Is it true that one cannot argue about taste? Is it improper, therefore, to speak of people of bad taste? Have there not been debates for years about the esthetic value of a considerable number of statues, paintings and poems? Are these discussions, then, futile, and is there no way of determining the value of an artistic work or the conduct of a person?

He who supports the thesis *de gustibus non disputandum* wishes to affirm a peculiar characteristic of value, i.e., the intimate and immediate nature of valuation. The pleasure produced in us by a glass of good wine, the reading of a poem, a prelude by Chopin, is something personal, intimate, private, and frequently, ineffable. We do not wish to relinquish this intimacy, for if we did, an essential part of esthetic enjoyment would then slip through our fingers. How can anyone convince us with syllogisms and learned quotations, when our pleasure is so immediate and direct that it does not admit any possibility of error?

However, if one does not take refuge in subjectivity, and tries to keep a cool head even though his heart is anything but calm, he will soon find that this doctrine is not satisfactory. What would become of ethical norms and esthetic masterpieces if each of us abided by his own particular way of looking at things? How can chaos be avoided, unless there are standards of value, norms of behavior? If every one carries his own yardstick of valuation, by what standard shall we decide axiological conflicts? Esthetic and moral education would be impossible; moral life will be meaningless; repentance of sin would seem absurd. "Moral" for whom? "Sin" for whom? one would have to ask constantly. On the other hand, if one were to measure esthetic value by the intensity of individual or collective emotion, greater value would accrue to screen or radio melodrama (which has such wide sentimental appeal) than to *Hamlet* or *King Lear*, which have appealed to a much smaller audience. If we make man the measure of esthetic value and moral law, it would appear that there would be, strictly speaking, neither "good taste" nor morality.

This issue is an old one. Indeed, it is as old as axiology itself, and the history of value theory could be written around this basic problem and the various solutions which have been proposed to solve it.

2. Are Values Objective or Subjective?

While it is not easy to reduce to simple terms the

constellation of problems with which axiology is
concerned today, the core of the problem may be summed
up in the following question: *Are things valuable because
we desire them, or do we desire them because they are
valuable?* Does desire, pleasure or interest give value to an
object, or are we interested because such objects possess a
value which is prior and foreign to our psychological and
organic reactions? Though in a different context, we find
the two attitudes in Shakespeare's *Troilus and Cressida*:
(II, 2):

> *Hector:* Brother, she is not worth what she doth cost
> The holding.
> *Troilus:* What is aught, but as 'tis valued?
> *Hector:* But value dwells not in particular will;
> It holds his estimate and dignity
> As well wherein 'tis precious of itself.

If one prefers a more technical and traditional way of
posing the problem, one may ask: Are values objective or
subjective?

The question requires prior clarification of terms in
order to prevent us from falling into a *disputatio de
nominem*. Value is "objective" if its existence and nature
is independent of a subject; conversely, it is "subjective" if
it owes its existence, its sense, or its validity, to the
feelings or attitudes of the subject.

An illustration can further clarify the sense of the
problem. As it has been pointed out, physical objects have
certain qualities, called "primary," which are inherent in
the objects themselves and others, such as sense or
"secondary" qualities, which depend at least partially
upon a subject who perceives them. To take a specific
value: which of these two types of qualities is beauty
closest to? Is it like length, which does not depend on the
subject? Or is it instead like smell, which in order to exist

requires the presence of a subject to perceive it, since an odor which no one can smell is nonexistent?

At times we lean toward subjectivism and we think we have discovered in the contrary point of view a mere delusion, similar to that suffered by the victim of hallucinations who is frightened by the phantoms created by his own imagination. On the other hand, there are times when it appears evident to us that values are objective realities to which we should submit, since they possess an overpowering force which brushes aside our preferences and overcomes our will. Do we not, at times, make efforts to create a work of art—a poem, a painting, a novel—only to give it up as a failure immediately we note that beauty is lacking in our creation? Something similar occurs when we appraise positively objects which we do not like, or when we notice the scant value of that which arouses us because of purely personal reasons.

But, returning to the first position, what values would objects have if we passed them by indifferently, if they did not cause us enjoyment or satisfaction, if we did not desire them, or were unable to desire them?

One point seems clear: we cannot speak of values without considering actual or possible valuations. In fact, what sense would values have if they could completely escape man's appreciation? How would we know that such values exist, if they existed outside the sphere of human valuation? In this point, subjectivism seems to be on firm ground; value cannot be divorced from valuation. Objectivism creates a basic distinction here which prevents us from pursuing the already open road of subjectivity. It is true, claims the objectivist, that valuation is subjective, but a distinction should be made between valuation and value. Value is prior to valuation. If there were no values, what would we evaluate? To confuse valuation with value is like confusing perception with the object perceived. Perception does not create the object; it grasps it. The same thing happens in the case of valuation. What is subjective is the apprehension of values, but values exist before being apprehended.

To show the weakness of this kind of reasoning, subjectivism appeals to experience. If values were objective, it asserts, then individuals would have come to an agreement about values, and value objects. But this is not the case; we find disagreement everywhere.

"Is there agreement concerning the basic principles of science?" retorts the objectivist. The mistakes made by certain persons do not invalidate the objectivity of truth. There are still people who believe in spontaneous generation and evil spirits. Truth does not depend on the opinion of individuals, but on the objectivity of facts; hence it cannot be strengthened nor weakened by the democratic procedure of counting votes. Similarly, in the case of values. The opinion of those of poor taste does not impair the beauty of a work of art. It would be idle to try to obtain unanimity of opinion. "But," the objectivist goes on to say, "there is still another point: the discrepancy refers to value objects, not to values. No one can fail to appreciate beauty; what may happen is that people may not recognize the presence of beauty in a certain object, whether this be a statue, a painting, or a symphony. Similarly, in the case of the other values: who can fail to appraise utility, prefer the pleasant, or appreciate honesty?"

"It is not so," the subjectivist will probably reply; "the disagreement referred to is extended to values themselves. When an Italian and an American disagree about the elegance of a pair of shoes, such an argument about a concrete object is due to a different manner of understanding elegance itself. Though it is true that sometimes we disagree about value objects, such disagreement frequently reveals a profound discrepancy between values such as beauty, justice or elegance."

"There are concrete instances," the subjectivist will go on to say, "which show clearly the subjectivity of values. Postage stamps constitute one such case. Where does the value of used stamps lie? Is there something in the quality of the paper, or in the beauty of the drawing, or in the print, which explains the value they have? They would have no value, were it not for the philatelists. Our desire to collect them is what has bestowed value upon them. If this interest is lost, the value which has been conferred upon them disappears *ipso facto*. Although the problem is somewhat more complex, something similar occurs in the case of esthetic values. They, too, depend on a series of conditions—subjective, cultural and sociological. What esthetic value would a painting have if men did not have eyes? And what sense would there be in talking about the esthetic value of music if God had condemned us to eternal deafness? In the last analysis, we value what we desire and what pleases us."

"Not so," replies the objectivist; "we value also that which displeases us. Who likes to risk his life to save a man who is drowning, especially if that man is our enemy? Nevertheless, we do it because it is the right thing to do. We place what is right above our pleasure or desire. Duty is objective and is based on a moral value which is equally so, and lies beyond the fluctuations of our likes and dislikes, interests, and desires. Or, to refer to a more ordinary type of illustration: who likes the dentist's "torture"? Nevertheless, we value his work. Is it pleasant to have a leg amputated? Displeasure notwithstanding, we are grateful to the man who amputates our leg when this would save our life. One must distinguish between valuation as a psychological act, and the truth of the valuation. As an experience, a wrong perception is as much a perception as a true one; yet we do not, on that account, equate the two when we judge the accuracy involved."

Such arguments are, for the subjectivists, a sample of

the superficiality of the analysis of their thesis. At first glance, it seems evident that the dentist is the cause of our pain, when he drills one of our teeth, and that consequently, the value which we ascribe to his work has nothing to do with pleasure, but is rather dictated by a higher concern. But the latter is also based on pleasure: we prefer a temporary pain for a few minutes to a prolonged toothache from a cavity. Or, if it is a matter of esthetic motivation that makes us willing to submit to torture in the dentist's chair (this, especially in the case of women) it is because we prefer the more lasting pleasure afforded by pleasant-looking teeth to the uncomfortable feeling brought on by the necessity of having to exhibit a sickly-looking set of teeth. The example of the leg amputation reveals even more sharply the confusion which we have indicated. We accept the pain of the leg amputation because it saves us from a greater pain. In both cases, we sacrifice temporary pleasure for a lasting one.

"One cannot formulate a theory based on two examples," argues the objectivist. "What satisfaction is derived by us through the act of saving the life of our enemy? Perhaps it may be argued that it is the satisfaction of having performed our duty. Our duty cannot be identified with what is pleasant; if this were so, everybody would perform his duty. Honesty depends on our capacity to overcome the claims of our pleasures, appetites and comforts. Pleasure operates on a low level of our personality, and we cannot sacrifice the highest (which is what moral values are) to the lowest. But even within the realm of the pleasant, it is necessary to distinguish between what pleases us and what we recognize as being pleasant. We frequently differentiate between what is pleasant and what we like because of personal or circumstantial motives. I still like to listen to an old waltz which used to move me when I was an adolescent; yet, I do not admit that it is more pleasant than, for example, Schubert's

Unfinished Symphony. Similarly, in the case of desire, it is necessary to separate what is desired from what is desirable. The fact that people desire something does not change it to something desirable. By the same token, I may not at the moment have the faintest desire to drink champagne, but I cannot fail to admit that it is a pleasant, desirable drink.

The subjectivist does not believe that one should postulate a world of the pleasant and desirable per se; both are related to real, specific pleasures and desires. When I admit that something is pleasant which, under different circumstances, I find unpleasant, this is not because I recognize an intrinsic quality, foreign to concrete experiences of pleasure. For example, if I recognize that champagne is pleasant, although it is unpleasant to drink it for breakfast, it is because I consider that on other occasions I like it. I am opposing two personal reactions: one transitory—which is the present—and another, more permanent; and not my personal reaction to the supposed objectivity of the value known as "pleasant." Anything that is pleasant in an object is derived from the pleasure which it calls forth. Could anything be pleasant if it did not please anybody, or if there were no possibility that it might please? The pleasant is a concept which is based on personal experiences of pleasure, and does not exist in a metaphysical world. If we sever the connections between pleasure and what is pleasurable, the latter disappears completely. Similar considerations would have to be granted in the case of the desired and the desirable. When we define the desirable as that which is worthy of being desired, we do not transfer the concept to a meta-empirical world; what we mean is that it would be desired by a person in "normal" circumstances. The example involving the postage stamps proves clearly that real and actual desire is what confers value upon things; when this is lacking, value disappears.

The subjectivist arguments do not succeed in convincing those who adhere to the objectivist thesis. The latter maintain that an entire axiological theory cannot be made to rest on an example involving postage stamps; an examination of any other case proves the opposite. "Hence," they repeat, "things do not have value because we desire them, but we desire them precisely because they are valuable. In fact, it would appear that we do not desire them out of sheer caprice, or without reason, but because something is within them which makes them *desirable* in the two senses of being capable and worthy of being desired."

3. Suggestions for a New Way of Looking at the Problem

Though the mind is enriched by the arguments offered by both sides, the discussion shows no sign of abating. Nor are the problems settled by deciding in favor of one or the other position. If we admit that value is of a subjective nature, there still remains to be decided just which aspect of subjectivity it is that gives value its force. Do objects possess value because they please us? Or perhaps because we desire them or we are interested in them? And why do we have an interest in certain things and not in others? Why do we like or prefer this to that? Is it an arbitrary psychological reaction or is there something in the object which compels us to react in a certain manner?

And so we land in the realm of objectivism. Nor are things crystal clear here. Is value completely alien to the biological and psychological constitution of man? Or is it true that all objectivity consists in the fact that man cannot fail to recognize value, once he is confronted by it? Isn't objectivity, possibly, of a completely different order? What about social objectivity, for example, in which the objectivity is based on the intersubjective character of the reaction? And once again, we are back to subjectivism.

This going around in circles, from one position to the opposite one, and then back again to the first, makes us think that perhaps the difficulty arises because the problem has been poorly stated. Does value necessarily have to be objective or subjective? Aren't we perhaps confused by our eagerness to reduce the whole to one of its essential elements? It is possible, for example, that pleasure, desire or interest, are a necessary but not a sufficient condition, and that they do not exclude objective elements. This is to say that value may be the result of a tension between the subject and the object, and therefore presents a subjective as well as an objective aspect, deceiving those who look only at one side of the coin.

We shall examine this possiblity in Chapter V. At the moment, let us attempt other paths. Do all values have identical character? The central problem concerns the nature of value. Should we not, before attempting to determine this, ask whether all values have a similar nature as concerns objectivity or subjectivity? Will not the element of subjectivity or objectivity vary according to the type of value? Let us explore this possibility for a moment, examining values which may belong to different hierarchies.

Let us begin with the lowest: those which pertain to pleasure or displeasure. I drink a glass of wine and find it pleasant. Where is the pleasant quality—in me or in the wine? Are we faced with a subjective or an objective value? It would seem that the pleasantness is a quality possessed by the wine, since Coca-Cola, for example, does not have the same pleasant effect. If I think a moment, I notice, nevertheless, that another person might be able to assert the exact opposite: that he likes Coca-Cola, and dislikes the wine. If this is so, it is not the object, but the subject

SCREW, B. 432
NEW YORK, N. Y

DEAR SIR

I'VE GOT
IDEA FOR
IS WORTH
IN YOUR
THIS WELL
WHO HEAV
& WHO IS
DRIVER GE
TOW A P
HIGH CENT
WOODSY
HE ENCOUN
FEMALE, T
WHO ALSO
INCREDIBL
WHILE HES
THE CHA
REAR BUM

.D   CHELSEA   STATION,
0011

HIS   INCREDIBLE
ARTICLE   I   FEEL
F   PUBLICATION
AZINE.   IN   IT,
IUNG   FELLOW,
/   INTO   SADISM
SO   A   TOW   TRUCK
A   CALL   TO
HE   THAT   LOT
ED   IN   A   QUIET,
I   ONCE,   THERE
IS   THIS   SULTRY
PORCHES   OWNER,
PENS   TO   HAVE
LARGE   BREASTS
RYING   TO   HOOK
UP   TO   THE
,   HE   ACCIDE

that is the source of value. If everyone reacts differently in the presence of the same stimulus, then the difference is probably traceable to the subject. It is not an acceptable refutation to say that there are people of poor taste who are incapable of enjoying wine, or whose taste has become perverted so that they find most pleasant what is not so. If we compare French and Italian wines, both of recognized quality, we notice that preferences are probably due to personal idiosyncrasies, or to habits acquired, from living in one country or the other. This is where the proverb *de gustibus non disputandum* makes sense, since it is a recognition of the predominance of the subjective over the objective on the lowest axiological level.

This predominance will be lost if we jump to the highest point on the axiological scale: to ethical values, for example. Is an attitude which we judge to be honest or dishonest, is a verdict just or unjust, dependent upon our feeling at the time? Of course not. We have to be above those subjective conditions which distort our ethical evaluation. What sort of judge would allow his verdicts to be affected by a stomach ache, or by the quarrels he might have had with his wife? Ethical value is so forceful that it compels us to acknowledge it, even against our personal desires and interests. At least, it appears that the element of objectivity is, in this sense, much greater than when we deal with what is pleasant.

Between these two extremes one finds other values: the useful, the vital, the esthetic. It is in the last group that the balance between the subjective and the objective appears greatest, although also varying according to the nature of the esthetic value. There is, for example, a predominance of the subjective element in evaluating an elegant dress—connected with fashion and other changing factors—which can be ignored when we evaluate the beauty of a painting.

4. The Methodological Problem

In recent years the impression has been gaining ground that the problem of the ultimate nature of value has entered an *impasse*. The history of science and philosophy has many times found itself face to face with a similar situation in which the main problem had to be postponed in order to give consideration to a prior problem. At the beginning of the 16th century, it was more important to find the means which would permit the discovery of new truths than to find the truths themselves. This was the contribution of Francis Bacon and Descartes, among others. Something similar occurred at the end of the 17th century when Locke put aside metaphysical questions in order first to pose the problem of the origin of our ideas; or a century later, when Kant made the nature of knowledge the central concern of theoretical philosophy to the detriment of the metaphysical problem.

In the face of the impossibility of settling the dispute between subjectivists and objectivists, many have thought that the moment has finally arrived when that question could be put aside in order to give priority to problems of method and criteria. What criteria shall we utilize to decide who is right? What is the most appropriate method of discovering the ultimate nature of value? John Dewey is one of the thinkers who believes that the main problem today is methodological. After having concerned himself with axiological questions for several decades, Dewey, at the age of 90, wrote: "In the present situation, as concerns the problem of values, the decisive question is of a methodological type." And Dewey is not alone; there are many who feel as he does, namely, that axiology will not emerge from the condition in which it finds itself, unless the problem of method is first clarified.

It is true that the method which is selected cannot be completely separated from the theoretical preferences, so that a course of action is already indicated in the statement of the problem; but it is no less true that if the criterion to be utilized is not determined with a certain degree of clarity, then the discussion is not only interminable but fruitless. On the other hand, an adequate method can shed a good deal of light on the problem, especially if the method does not carry with it an advance commitment to a definite theory.

Which is the road, then, to be followed? Two chief possibilities open up before us: one is empirical, the other a priori. Will we have to adjust to experience and abide by its decisions, or should we trust emotional intuition, as Scheler would prefer—capable of transporting us to the very intimacy of essence and assuring us of unquestionable knowledge?

Experience is the supreme judge in matters of fact; it will tell us, if we wish to undertake a complicated research problem, what people really prefer, what they really value, and what they dislike. But on the basis of the observation that people value in a certain manner, we cannot infer by way of conclusion that this is the way in which they should value. We have already seen that if we made value dependent upon facts, there would be no possibility for moral reform, since moral law would be identified with the mores of a given community. The essence of the moral reformer and of the creator in the field of art lies in not adjusting to the predominant norms or tastes, but unfurling the flag of what "ought to be" over and above people's preferences.

Are we left, then, only with the other alternative, that of infallible intuition, which asserts haughtily and not very philosophically that those who disagree with its theories have "value blindness"? What should we do if the infallible intuitions of two of these "chosen few" do not agree? And what should we think of the infallibility of intuition when it is the same individual—as is the case with Scheler himself—who, in the course of his life, experienced "infallible" intuitions which are contradictory?

These difficulties reveal to us a characteristic peculiar to philosophy. Scientific propositions, (however difficult) are judged true or false according to commonly agreed-upon criteria. One can stand firmly on this foundation upon which science rests. On the other hand, in philosophy, the criterion to be utilized, the yardstick, is also a problem under discussion. There is no yardstick to measure the yardstick. This should not cast us into the depths of despair or scepticism; it should reveal to us the complexity of philosophic problems, and make us cautiously alert to over-simplified solutions which settle problems by pushing them aside. The philosophical attitude is basically problem oriented. He who is not capable of grasping the sense of problems and who prefers to seize upon the first solution which presents itself, and which offers him illusory stability, runs the risk of being drowned in a sea of difficulties. It is because no axiological theory can be understood without first grasping the essence of the problems which that theory endeavors to solve, that we have devoted this chapter to problems of present-day value theory. But this is not the end of the dilemma. The problems indicated are the most important, but they are not the only ones. Before passing on to the proposed solutions, it would be best to glance at some other axiological problems. Since it is impossible to present them all, we shall single out those which appear to have the greatest significance.

5. How Do We Apprehend Values?

Let us limit the methodological problem to the smaller, yet no less important question of the apprehension of values. How do we grasp values?

We have seen in Chapter I that values are not self-sustaining, but that they lead a parasitical existence; they always appear to us, resting on some carrier, or value object. This carrier is a real object—stone, canvas, paper, gesture, movement—and we perceive it through the senses. Do we perceive in the same way the value which rests on it? Let us not confuse the question: it is evident that if we do not perceive the object via the senses, in which the value is embodied, the value will be concealed from us. The question which we pose is different. We want to know whether it is through the senses or via any other means that we perceive the values once embodied. Thus, for example, when we see two apples, we perceive each one with our eyes; the similarity, however, is perceived not with the eyes of our face, but with those of our mind. It is evident that it would not have been possible to perceive the similarity intellectually, if we had not first seen the objects. This truth does not exclude the former. The same thing happens in the case of values: we can, and we should, separate the perception of real objects which serve as a vehicle for values, from the values themselves, and ask ourselves if both are perceived in a similar manner.

Aside from the interest which the problem of the perception of values offers by itself, its solution will shed light on the nature of the values themselves. Since we cannot ourselves penetrate the very being of objects "in themselves," by eliminating our own person, we ought to resign ourselves to discovering the nature of objects according to the relationship we bear to them. Thus, for example, the difference that exists between *a* horse, *the* horse (as species or essence), and a centaur, is a consequence of what we can do with them. We can see, lasso, ride *a* horse; we cannot do the same with *the* horse or with a centaur. We can imagine the centaur, but we cannot touch it; *the* horse cannot be imagined, nor touched. Of what disposition, race, age, sex, can *the* horse be? Since it does not possess any of these characteristics, we cannot imagine it; we can, on the other hand, think of it. Because we are capable only of thinking of it, and not riding it we know that *the* horse is a concept, and not a real living animal.

The relationship, then, or the dealings we have with an object, reveal its nature to us. Well, then, what can we do with values?

Max Scheler maintains that intelligence is blind to values, i.e., it cannot have any sort of direct dealing with them. Values are revealed to us, according to the widespread theory of this German philosopher, through emotional intuition. Intuition is accurate and has no need to base itself on prior experience, nor on its corresponding vehicle. "We know of cases in the apprehension of values," he writes, "in which the value of a thing is given to us clearly and evidently, even *without* having the *carriers* of that value revealed to us."[1] José Ortega y Gasset, who made known Scheler's axiological conception to the Spanish-speaking world, wrote in 1923:

> The experience of values is independent of the experience of things. Moreover, it is of quite a different sort. Objects, realities, are by nature *opaque* to our perception. There is no way whereby we can ever see an apple in its entirety: we have to turn it, open it, divide it, and we shall never get to perceive it wholly. Our experience of it will continually improve, but it will never be perfect. On the other hand, the unreal—a number, a triangle, a concept, a value—is a *transparent* entity. We see them all at once in their entirety.[2]

Do we really perceive values at first sight and in their

1. Max Scheler, *Der Formalismus in der Ethik und die materiale Wertethik* (Bern: Francke-Verlag, 1954), p. 40.

2. J. Ortega y Gasset, *Obras completas*, Vol. VI (Madrid: Revista de Occidente, 1947), p. 333.

entirety? Are they really transparent? Are they revealed to us through emotional intuition?

The experience of artists, of art critics and historians, does not coincide with this optimistic description of the perception of value. A long and painful process is necessary at times for the work of art to disclose its previously hidden beauty. The grasp is never definitive; new approaches will afford us new surprises. In the realm of ethics, things are even more complicated. The honesty of one's behavior, or the injustice of a verdict, is not evident to us at first glance, and sometimes not even after long consideration.

We must be on our guard against the emotional character of the supposedly intuiting of value. Even within the esthetic realm, where the emotional aspect appears to predominate, there are intellectual elements which form part of our apprehension. If we proceed from the esthetic to the ethical or legal, the presence of rational elements is undeniable. When considering what is useful, reason takes the place of emotions. The utility of an object cannot be apprehended without a prior concept of the purpose which it is to fulfill, and the manner in which it fulfills it.

On the other hand, if it were true that we grasp values completely and intuitively, what should we do in the face of contradictory intuitions? There is not the slightest doubt that such intuitions exist. To say that one whose intuition is different from ours is blind to values implies arrogance and a lack of critical spirit; the clash of intuitions occurs in individuals of similar abilities. Which intuition will put an end to the intuitive contradiction?

These observations mean to point out the difficulties which every axiological theory should face up to, and the impossibility of eliminating the difficulties merely by affirming a point of view dogmatically. The problem remains wide open. The important thing is to understand the meaning, depth and complexity of the issue. Such understanding will prevent us from adopting a dogmatic doctrine, or from becoming disoriented in the face of contradictory theories which claim to be true and are supported by facts and reasons of similar weight.

6. Bibliography

BAIER, Kurt. *The Moral Point of View*. Ithaca: Cornell University Press, 1958. See Chap. I.

DEWEY, John. *Problems of Men*. New York: Philosophical Library, 1946. See Part III.

————. *Theory of Valuation*. International Encyclopedia of Unified Science, Vol. II, No. 4. Chicago: The University of Chicago Press, 1939.

FINDLAY, J. N. *Values and Intentions: A Study in Value Theory and Philosophy of Mind*. London: Allen and Unwin, 1961.

FRONDIZI, Risieri. "The Axiological Foundation of Moral Norm." *The Personalist*, Vol. 50, No. 2 (Spring, 1969), 241-53.

LAIRD, John. *The Idea of Value*. Cambridge: Cambridge University Press, 1929.

LAMONT, W. D. *The Value Judgement*. Edinburgh: Edinburgh University Press, 1955.

LEWIS, Clarence I. *An Analysis of Knowledge and Valuation*. La Salle, Illinois: The Open Court Publishing Co., 1946. See Book III.

LORING, L. M. *Two Kinds of Values*. London: Routledge & Kegan Paul, 1966. See Chaps. I and II.

PEPPER, Stephen. *The Source of Value*. Berkeley: The University of California Press, 1958.

SESONSKE, Alexander. *Value and Obligation: The Foundations of an Empiricist Ethical Theory*. New York: Oxford University Press, 1964.

The
Subjectivist
Doctrines

1. Beginning of Axiology

Alexius Meinong (1853-1921) was the first to state, in systematic form, the subjectivist interpretation of values, in his work entitled *Psychological-ethical Inquiry into a Theory of Value.*[1] Nevertheless, he was not the initiator of axiology, as some authors have claimed.

Two outstanding British philosophers can be mentioned as antecedents of the subjective interpretation of value. Thomas Hobbes (1588-1679) maintains in his *Leviathan*, (Part I, Chapter 6):

> Whatsoever is the object of any man's appetite or desire, that is it which he for his part calls *good*; and the object of his hate and aversion, *evil*; and of his contempt, *vile* and *inconsiderable*. For these words of good, evil, and contemptible, are ever used with relation to the person that uses them, there being nothing simply and absolutely so; nor any common rule of good and evil to be taken from the nature of the objects themselves.

When David Hume (1711-1776) is trying to prove that the distinction between virtue and vice does not derive from reason, he argues this way in his famous *Treatise*:

> Take any action allowed to be vicious: wilful murder, for instance. Examine it in all lights and see if you can find the matter of fact, or real existence, which you call *vice*. In whichever way you take it, you find only certain passions, motives, volitions and thoughts. There is no other matter of fact in the case. The vice entirely escapes you, as long as you consider the object. You never can find it, till you turn your reflexion into your own breast, and find a sentiment of disapprobation, which arises in you towards this action. Here is a matter of fact; but it is the object of feeling, not of reason. It lies in yourself, not in the object. So that when

1. *Psychologisch-ethische Untersuchungen zur Werttheorie* (Graz: Leuschner u. Lubensky, 1894).

you pronounce any action or character to be vicious, you mean nothing, but that from the constitution of your nature you have a feeling or sentiment of blame from the contemplation of it. Vice and virtue, therefore, may be compared to sounds, colours, heat and cold, which, according to modern philosophy, are not qualities in objects, but perceptions in the mind.[2]

His opinion is the same about aesthetic values. He writes that "Beauty is no quality in things themselves; it exists merely in the mind which contemplates them; and each mind perceives a different beauty."[3]

On the other hand, the great rationalist continental philosopher Baruch Spinoza (1632-1677) maintains a similar doctrine in his *Ethics* (III, Prop. IX, Schol):

> In no case do we strive for, wish, desire or long for anything because we deem it to be good, but on the contrary, we deem a thing to be good, because we strive for, wish, desire or long for it.[4]

Setting aside these and other antecedents which might be found in ancient, medieval and modern philosophy,[5] it must be admitted that the economists and in particular Adam Smith (1723-1790), were the first to interest

2. D. Hume, *Treatise of Human Nature*, Book III, Part I, Sect. 1, Selby-Bigge edition, pp. 468-69.

3. D. Hume, *Essays Literary, Moral and Political*, Essay XXII: "Of the Standard of Taste" (Green-Grose, 1898), p. 268.

4. The same opinion is usually found in literature and in people who have no knowledge of philosophy. Shakespeare wrote in *Hamlet* (II, 2, 252-53): "There is nothing either good or bad, but thinking makes it so," which is reminiscent of Euripedes in *Aeolus*: "What shame is there but thinking makes it so?"

5. For some other antecedents, see Louis Lavelle, *Traité des Valeurs*, Vol. I (Paris: Presses Universitaires des France, 1951), Book I, Part 2, pp. 33-91; and R. Müller-Freienfels, *Metaphysik des Irrationalen* (1927), pp. 364-433.

themselves in values. But these concerns were limited to the field of political economy.

Among the philosophers, it is the German, H. Lotze (1817-1881), who took the lead in the study of values. When Positivism tried to establish a reality free of values, which would make possible the rigorous application of naturalistic methods, Lotze made values independent of reality. This conception helped him to delineate an area that would be guarded against any invasion of naturalism and to introduce in this way, the distinction between being and value, with its famous assertion, that values have no being, they simply have value. The importance which Lotze assigned to values was so great that he attempted to reduce logic, ethics and metaphysics to axiology.

The introduction of the notion of value made possible the separation of the social sciences, then in the embryonic stage, from the natural sciences since we cannot ignore value in the former. As a result of this separation, the imperialist attempts of naturalist positivism were side-stepped, since nature was foreign to value, and consequently, the methods of the natural sciences would not be applicable to any reality wherein value assumed first-class importance. This was the task of the Baden school, particularly of W. Windelband (1848-1915), influenced by Lotze, and of his successor at the University of Heidelberg, H. Rickert (1863-1936), well known for his *Kulturwissenschaft und Naturwissenschaft.*

Shortly before these scientific-philosophical studies, F. Nietzsche (1844-1900), converted values into the vital and passionate issue of the period. Nietzsche proclaimed the necessity for the "transmutation of values" which would allow for the upsurge of a new human culture, a substitute for the civilization which he called Christian. He interpreted the dynamic sense of history as a continuous creation and annihilation of values. These values, created by man, are stabilized and are in effect only temporarily, each being replaced subsequently by another. It is true that Nietzsche's thinking expressed itself in violent and paradoxical formulas which could be crystallized into a rigorous axiological doctrine only with great difficulty, but it is equally true that it was he who transformed the question of values into a passionate theme at the close of the century.

It is necessary to pass from Germany into Austria in order to be able to observe at close range the development of the first stages of axiology, and in particular, the formation of the subjectivist thesis.

We have already mentioned Meinong, initiator of the subjectivist doctrine. However, his philosophy is incomprehensible unless one first becomes acquainted with the doctrine of his teacher, Franz Brentano (1837-1917). Brentano was the source of the most influential streams of German thought. Meinong and Ehrenfels were his disciples. Husserl, the founder of phenomenology, was inspired by him, and particularly by his doctrine of intentionality. Husserl's influence, in turn, reached the greatest German-speaking philosophers of recent times, two of them the strongest supporters of objectivist doctrine: Max Scheler and Nicolai Hartmann.

Meinong and Ehrenfels, the first champions of subjectivism, were disciples of Brentano at the University of Vienna. The latter, however, was not a subjectivist; on the contrary, he maintained that values are objective.

Brentano established the bases of phenomenology with his research into the intentionality of consciousness. Although this characteristic of consciousness was known to the Scholastics, and there are even glimmerings of it in Aristotle, Saint Anselm and Abelard, it is Brentano (and later Husserl) who discovered the importance of intentionality. The intentionality of consciousness would eventually permit Brentano to pass from the psychic phenomena to the objects of such phenomena. Strangely enough, Brentano was the point of departure for the subjectivism developed by Meinong and Ehrenfels, and of Scheler's absolute objectivism.

Meinong gave the first subjectivist answer to the problem of the nature of value. As a disciple of Brentano, Meinong sought in the domain of psychology the key to the problem of values, and believed that the latter should be rooted in emotional life. He formulated a thesis which was to last until the present, but which he was to abandon by evolving gradually toward the opposite position. Meinong said: something has value when it pleases us, and to the extent to which it pleases us. This was the thesis which Christian von Ehrenfels (1850-1932), a follower of Meinong, was to criticize. Ehrenfels was to inaugurate, by means of his criticism, a famous controversy in the history of axiology, notable for the friendly and yet critical spirit which enlivened it.

2. The Polemic Between Meinong and Ehrenfels

This exemplary discussion which has resulted in an enrichment of subjectivist teaching—by placing in opposition the opinions of two men who start from a similar point of view but who part company upon selecting the aspect of subjectivity which gives validity to value—this discussion did not really originate with Meinong's work mentioned above, since Ehrenfels, a year earlier, in 1893, had published a work entitled *Werttheorie und Ethik* [6] *(Theory of Values and Ethics)*. Of course, Ehrenfels did not claim priority for the ideas contained in this work, since they had been collected in Meinong's

---

6. *Vierteljahrsschrift für wissenschaftliche Philosophie.*

seminars. The latter attempted to solve these differences, and in 1895 published an essay entitled *Über Werthalten und Wert*[7] *(On Evaluation and Value)*, to which Ehrenfels issued a rejoinder the following year in an article, published in the same journal, which he called *Von der Wertdefinition zum Motivationgesetze (From the Definition of Value to the Law of Motivation)*.

A year later, there appeared the first volume of the famous work by Ehrenfels, *System der Werttheorie*[8] *(System of the Theory of Values)* and the following year, the second volume[9] in whose appendix we find an echo of this polemic, a magnificent example of creative differences of opinion.

Every fruitful discussion implies that the difference rests on an agreement concerning basic issues. When the disagreement is complete, the dialogue becomes impossible, and the controversy turns out to be sterile. Meinong and Ehrenfels not only shared the same subjectivist orientation; they also had the same teacher, Brentano, not to mention their friendly personal and academic relationship.

Reduced to its simplest terms, the discussion can be summarized as follows: Meinong held in his *Psychological-ethical Inquiry* that it is necessary to start from valuation as a psychic fact. When we examine such a psychic fact, we find that it belongs to the realm of emotional life, that it is a sentiment. In accordance with Brentano's theory concerning the faculty of judgment as a postulation of the existence or nonexistence of an object, Meinong maintains that such sentiment is of existence.

---

7. *Archiv für systm. Philos.*

8. Vol. I.: *Allgemeine Werttheorie* (Leipzig: Reisland, 1897).

9. Vol. II.: *Grundzüge einer Ethik* (Leipzig: Reisland, 1898).

Consequently, in every valuation there is implicit a judgment which affirms or denies the existence of an object; based on this judgment, we experience pain or pleasure. Value is really a subjective state of an emotional nature, but reference to the object is maintained by means of existential judgment. Meinong writes that "an object has value insofar as it possesses the capacity for furnishing an effective basis for a value sentiment."[10]

Ehrenfels is quick to point out that Meinong's thesis suffers from one serious weakness. If an object is valuable when it is capable of producing in us a feeling of pleasure, then only existing things will be valuable. The truth is that we also value what does not exist; perfect justice, the moral good which is never realized. For this reason, Ehrenfels. doesn't think that the basis of values can be found in pleasure, but rather, one must look for it in the realm of appetite or desire. Things which we desire or covet are valuable, and they are so because we desire and covet them.

The shift in the basis of values from pleasure to desire does not imply, of course, a substantial modification of the subjectivist thesis, but it permits Meinong to make several objections which will force his colleague to readjust his doctrine. Actually, Meinong maintains that the value of an object cannot depend on whether it is desired, since one desires what one does not possess, and yet we value existing things which we already possess, such as the painting we have in our room, the wealth we have accumulated in the course of our life and the friends we have.

In the face of this objection, Ehrenfels admits the need for re-examining his theory, but without abandoning the basic principle. We value certain existent things, he replies,

10. *Psychologisch-ethische Untersuchungen zur Werttheorie*, p. 25.

because we think that if they did not exist, or if we did not possess them, we would desire them. This change makes it possible for him to propose a new definition: value is a relationship between a subject and an object which, by virtue of a clear and complete picture of the being of the object, determines within us, along the entire range of our feelings from pleasure to pain, an emotional condition more intense than its nonexistence of that very same object.

With this definition, he approaches the theory of Meinong, who in turn is also disposed to recognize his error in this process of mutual understanding. Meinong admits that we value also the nonexistent, but that on appraising it, we mean to assert that if the object ever existed, it would call forth in us a feeling of pleasure. Meinong differentiates between a value experienced at the moment and one that is potential. The first is contained in the object which is present and the second is possessed by that same object when the latter is absent. The value of an object, writes Meinong, consists in its ability to determine the emotional reaction of the subject, not only by virtue of the existence of the object, but also by its nonexistence. He recognizes the existence of a conflict of motives within consciousness and with this recognition he moves closer to Ehrenfels, since value would probably consist in the capacity which an object possesses to stimulate desire in the course of that conflict of motives. Meinong does not thereby abandon his fundamental thesis, namely, that pleasure is the ultimate basis of value.

The last echo of the controversy is found in the appendix to the second volume of Ehrenfels' work, already mentioned, *System of the Theory of Values* (1898), wherein he defines value as the relationship, falsely objectivized by language, between an object and the subject's desire for it, which would make him covet it, if its existence were to become uncertain.

Thus ends the polemic between these two famous Austrian philosophers.[11] With the dawn of the present century, the interests of each diverge and follow different paths. Ehrenfels abandons the field of axiology in order to devote himself to psychological research upon becoming associated with the University of Prague; in this connection, he became famous as a pioneer of *Gestalt* psychology. Meinong, on the other hand, continues his axiological research which, through the influence of his well-known theory of objects, will finally adopt a position contrary to that of his initial subjectivism.

3. Axiological Subjectivism in the Twentieth Century

Meinong's "conversion" to objectivism seemed to many German philosophers to be a sign of the right road which axiology ought to follow. It was believed that psychologism and the empiricism which sustained it, belonged to the past and that it was impossible to revive what was already buried. The famous refutation which Husserl delivered against psychologism in Volume I of his *Logical Investigations* marked the beginning of the demise in the German philosophy not only of psychologism, but of every form of empiricism. The new era of absolute truth was ushered in; relativistic thinking was no longer applicable. In the opinion of many German philosophers, rock bottom had finally been reached, thanks to phenomenology, and the solid edifice of philosophy began to be erected on a firm foundation.

---

11. About this famous polemic and the historical background, see Howard O. Eaton, *The Austrian Philosophy of Values* (Norman: University of Oklahoma Press, 1930) especially Chapter VIII.

Scheler's axiological doctrine which we shall examine in the next chapter took its departure from this hypothesis which went unchallenged in Germany in the first quarter of the century. That assurance was transmitted to Ibero America by the *Revista de Occidente*, and with regard to values, by Ortega y Gasset himself, who eventually wrote the following, considered to be the indisputable truth:

> The unreal—a number, a triangle, a concept, a value—is a *transparent* entity. We see them at once, in their entirety. Successive deliberations provide us with the most minute details, but it is during the first glance that they afford us their entire structure [. . . .] Hence, mathematics is an *a priori* science of absolute truths. Well, then, axiology or theory of values is likewise a system of evident and unchangeable truths, of a type similiar to mathematics.[12]

Subjectivism soon became in Germany, Spain and Latin America the doctrine of the novices, and there was not a manual or dictionary of philosophy which did not speak of the objectivity of values as a characteristic accepted without question by contemporary axiology.

Just as the human spirit possesses great capacity to react against the decadent forms of scepticism and pessimism, because it cannot do without the positive, creative and fruitful feeling which stimulates it, so it similarly resists being trapped definitely by a dogmatism which resolves all problems with emphatic assertions. The creative sense saves it from the first danger; the critical spirit, from the second.

When the German-speaking world, which had monopolized axiology almost completely, discarded the subjectivistic thesis quite definitely to all intents and purposes, the latter re-appeared with renewed vigor in the English-speaking world. It is not by chance that this should

12.   Ortega y Gasset, *Obras completas* (Madrid: *Revista de Occidente,* 1947), VI, p. 333.

have arisen precisely in this area; it was here that the radical forms of political and religious individualism acquired maturity; the nominalist and empiricist tradition initiated by William of Occam and Francis Bacon was never lost. William James was right when he stated that there is a philosophical thread which leads directly from Hume to contemporary empiricism via J. S. Mill, and which leaves aside Kant with his a priori, as well as the great systems of post-Kantian idealism. The assertion is true, at least as concerns the thinking of the English-speaking peoples, who have always looked with suspicion upon any attempt at a priori knowledge and at the existence of metaempirical entities.

It is true that among the first North American axiologists, the objectivists predominate. One of the first was Wilbur M. Urban, author in 1909 of an important work entitled *Valuation, Its Nature and Laws*.[13] It is no less true that Urban and the objectivism of idealistic origin represented the transplantation of foreign thought, specifically that of German origin.[14]

When in Great Britain and in the United States, there arises a reaction against this idealism of Germanic origin (when the polemic against F. H. Bradley and Josiah Royce is initiated) English thought again emphasizes its empirical tradition. And as soon as the problem of values is

---

13. (London-New York: Macmillan, 1909). Since then, Urban published numerous articles on axiology.

14. German influence was due not only to the fact that the chief representatives of philosophical thought at the beginning of the century studied in Germany (Royce, B. P. Bowne, Hocking, etc.) but also to the arrival of some German philosophers. According to R. B. Perry, the North Americans "heard of 'walues' before they heard of 'values'," (*Realms of Value*, p. 4), due to the Germanic pronunciation of Hugo Münsterberg (1863-1916), who, as professor at Harvard University at the beginning of the century, was one of those who introduced value theory into the United States.

carried over into the field of experience, it is placed on the road which leads to subjectivism.[15]

The development of value theory, both in America and Great Britain, is part of the general evolution of philosophy in both places. The new tendencies in axiology are related to the two movements characteristic of contemporary American philosophy: realism and pragmatism. As is well known, both movements arise as a reaction against Royce's idealism. In England, a neo-realist movement appears which runs parallel to the American, beginning with the famous article by G. E. Moore, entitled *The Refutation of Idealism*, published in the journal, *Mind*, in 1903.

In the United States the reaction began with William James's article, *Does Consciousness Exist?* published in 1904. Other articles by William James, and the publication in 1910 of the *Program and First Platform of Six Realists*, which gave rise to the movement known as neo-realism, showed clearly that the supremacy of idealism was beginning to decline in the United States.

The six young men[16] who were favorably inclined toward the neo-realist movement, upheld both epistemological realism and the necessity of adopting a method similar to that of scientists. In the first place, they pointed out that problems should be isolated and examined one by one; moreover, they indicated that the solitary efforts of the traditional philosopher ought to be

---

15. One should not allow oneself to be deceived by labels: axiological subjectivism is related to epistemological realism, and not to idealism as might be thought. R. B. Perry, B. Russell, and so many other English-speaking philosophers prove it clearly. Contemporary American and English idealism was an absolute idealism *a la* Hegel, and not subjective and empirical, as in Berkeley; it has therefore upheld the objective and absolute character of values.

16. W. P. Montague, R. B. Perry, E. B. Holt, W. T. Marvin, E. G. Spaulding, and G. B. Pitkin.

replaced by groups working as a team, as the scientists were doing.[17] The general attitude of the group was empiricist, and all of its members looked with favor upon the development of the new forms of American psychology.

4. R. B. Perry and Value as an Object of Interest

It is precisely one of these young neo-realists, R. B. Perry, who formulates the first and most outstanding subjectivist theory in the field of contemporary American axiology.

Ralph Barton Perry (1876-1957), was a disciple of Royce and James at Harvard University. At the age of 25, he published an article refuting the thesis of his idealist teacher, and soon found intellectual support in William James who was to become a friend for the rest of his life. Once the controversy against idealism died down, Perry put aside his concern with epistemology and became interested in ethical and axiological questions.

The same year (1926) in which Nicolai Hartmann published his famous *Ethik* in Berlin, wherein he upheld the extreme theory of axiological objectivism, R. B. Perry

17. They put this idea into practice when they published, in 1912, a book in which all collaborated, entitled *The New Realism: Cooperative Studies in Philosophy*.

published his *General Theory of Value*, in which he defends a subjectivist position that still enjoys great prestige in the United States.[18] In this lengthy work on values, Perry ignores the objectivist theories and looks for the origin and basis of value in subjective experience. He soon finds that *interest* is the key factor. But the relation of interest and value could be of different kinds. In the first place, interest could be aroused by some element in the object that makes it desirable or interesting. In the second place, value may be assigned to objects of certain qualified interests; and finally value may be derived from any kind of interest about any object. How shall we then conceive the relation? Should it be by analogy with the magnet and the iron-filing, in which case the object draws the interest to itself? In this case, value would be the capacity to command interest. Or should we conceive it by the analogy with a target? Anything may become a target when anyone aims at it. In this case value would spring from interest, and is conferred to the object just because we happen to have interest in it. Perry maintains this last doctrine which is the most extreme position.

He expressly rejects the doctrine that value depends on a "qualified object of interest" as well as the opposite doctrine that maintains that value depends upon a "qualified interest"[19] to hold his own view that any interest whatsoever confers value upon any object of any

18. Besides the two outstanding works in axiology and numerous articles on the most diverse philosophical themes, Perry published the following books: *The Approach to Philosophy* (1905); *The Moral Economy* (1909); *Present Philosophical Tendencies* (1912); *The Present Conflict of Ideals* (1918); *Philosophy of the Recent Past* (1926); *The Thought and Character of William James* (1935); *In the Spirit of William James* (1938); *Shall not Perish from the Earth* (1940); *Puritanism and Democracy* (1944); *Characteristically American* (1949).

19. *General Theory of Value* (2d ed.; Cambridge, Mass.: Harvard University Press, 1950), Chap. III and IV.

kind. "That which is an object of interest is *eo ipso* invested with value. Any object whatever it be, acquires value when any interest, whatever it be, is taken in it."[20]

Twenty-eight years later, in a new book on values, entitled *Realms of Value*, Perry reiterates his conception of value as that which is an object of interest. He expresses himself in terms which reassert his previous formulations:

"A thing—anything—has value, or is valuable, in the original and generic sense when it is the object of an interest—any interest. Or, whatever is object of interest is ipso facto valuable." [21]

Consequently, the following equation may be formulated: "*x* is valuable=interest is taken in *x*."[22]

If any kind of interest confers value upon any kind of object, be it real or imaginary, the concept of interest acquires singular importance in axiology. Perry has concerned himself with this in a careful study which the reader will be able to read with profit in the *General Theory*.[23]

Interest, according to Perry, has to do with the whole affective-motor life and should not be limited to its ordinary meaning. In many cases, this term can be replaced by *desire, will, purpose*. It does not, of course, have the customary meaning of "curiosity" or of an "object capable of provoking curiosity" (interesting); rather, it seeks to express the complex attitude of every living being when it finds itself in favor of or opposed to certain things. It

20. *Ibid.*, pp. 115-16.

21. *Realms of Value, A Critique of Human Civilization* (Cambridge, Mass.: Harvard University Press, 1954), p. 3.

22. *General Theory of Value*, p. 116.

23. See especially the chapters dealing with the biological aspect of interest (Chapter VI), the psychological definition of interest (Chapter VII), and the modes of interest (Chapters VIII-X).

includes, therefore, both desire and aversion, seeking and avoiding, pleasure and displeasure; on the other hand, interest does not relate only to the condition, but also to the act, disposition or attitude in favor of or against something.[24] It is this pro-attitude which confers value on an object. *"In the last analysis good springs from desire and not desire from good."*[25] The relationship of "interest" to the whole effective-motor life reveals Perry's preference for "scientific" psychology and rejection of the Cartesian dualism of body and soul.[26]

Perry appears to leave completely aside the qualities of the object itself, which are capable of calling forth within us the interest which makes the object valuable. "The silence of the desert is without value until some wanderer finds it lonely and terrifying; the cataract, until some human sensibility finds it sublime."[27]

Why does the traveler find the desert lonely and terrifying and the waterfall sublime? Is it not because the desert possesses qualities different from those of the waterfall, and that in its presence, we cannot fail to react in a manner likewise different? Of course, the desert would not be terrifying if there were not any men capable of being terrified, but we cannot deduce from this fact that we confer that character upon the desert when we become terrified.[28] Pigeons can inspire terror in a neurotic; yet

---

24. *General Theory*, p. 27, especially note 1; and Section 49, p. 115; see also *Realms of Value*, p. 3.

25. *General Theory*, p. 116, n. 5.

26. *Ibid.*, pp. 142-45.

27. *Ibid.*, p. 125.

28. Perry seems to make the logical mistake common to this type of reasoning: "If one cannot find the experience of terror unless there is a subject who is terrified, the terrifying experience depends only on the subject." He ignores the possibility that it is a relational notion.

this fact does not permit us to assert that pigeons are terrifying. There is in Perry, as in many other subjectivists, an exaggeration of the errors of axiological objectivism, in favor of his own doctrine. The correct assertion that nothing can be terrifying if there is no subject to appraise it, can only lead one to infer legitimately that the subject who appraises cannot be discarded when one examines the nature of value.

On the other hand, every exclusively psychological definition will, moreover, have to face the difficulties which arise when one wishes to identify what is "good" with psychological reaction. If we interpret Perry's definition literally, namely, that anything has value when it is the object of any interest whatsoever, we would not be able to have dishonest or sinful interests. The truth is that we do have them, and that in the realm of ethics one would have to add to interest a qualifier of a moral nature; there would be bad interests as well as good ones. In such a case, the psychological definition is of very little use, since the really important element is provided by the qualifier which is added to it.

If the adjective which gives value to the object is missing, it would be impossible to determine what is "better," since "better" implies "good." Perry does not share this thesis and tries to determine the hierarchy of values with criteria which have to do with the interpretation of the values themselves. "Value consists, as we have seen, in the relation which an object sustains to favorable or unfavorable interest, and if an object can be said to be better or worse this must be because the relation in question determines these differences. It is the interest which confers value on the object, and it must also be interest which confers the amount of the value."[29] Perry

29. *Ibid.*, p. 599. He discusses the heirarchy of values—that he calls commensurability—in Chapter XXI.

proposes three criteria; intensity, preference and inclusiveness.[30] An object, for example, wine, is better than another object, for example, water, if (i) the interest in wine is more intense than the interest in water; (ii) if wine is preferred to water, and (iii) if the interest in wine is more inclusive than the interest in water.[31]

Perry maintains that these criteria have been recognized by philosophy as well as by common sense. The Hedonist school has emphasized the principle of intensity, humanism that of preference, and moral austerity that of inclusiveness. The three principles are independent in the sense that they cannot be *reduced one to another* and, in his opinion, they should be taken into consideration by every theory which endeavors to set up valid standards concerning comparative value objects. *Intensity* makes possible the comparison of the several phases of the same interest in the same object; *preference* makes possible the comparison of the several objects of the same interest; and *inclusiveness* makes possible the comparison of the objects of one interest with the objects of another without the introduction of a third interest and it is the only standard by which all interest can be brought into one system having a maximum in all three respects or on the whole.[32]

Evil may be measured by the same standard used for *good*, since it is relative to magnitudes of negative interest. Therefore, an object is worse than another when the negative interest in it is more intense. In the second place, one thing is worse than another when we prefer not to have the former. He who "prefers the lesser pain" does not

---

30. These criteria correspond to the intensive, distensive and extensive magnitudes, indicated by W. E. Johnson in his *Logic*, Part II, Chapter VII, as Perry himself admits. See *General Theory*, p. 615, n. 37.

31. Perry, *General Theory*, Sect. 248, espec. p. 616.

32. *Ibid.*, p. 658; cf. also my footnote 24, this chapter.

desire pain at all; he just prefers the negation of great pain to the negation of little.

In the third place, b is worse than a when the negative interest in b is more inclusive than the negative interest in a. An object which is loathed by L and M is worse, other things being equal, than an object which is loathed only by L, or only by M.[33]

Perry's theory seems to be a good psychological interpretation of why we value something but a poor doctrine of what value is. It is true that we actually do not value something unless we like it, desire it, or have an interest in it, but we may interpret value as what is valuable, namely, what is desirable or worthy of being desired. If, as Perry wants, we try to reduce the desirable to the desired, what is interesting to what people are interested in, one should ask: whose interest is more valuable? A child's interest or his father's? A maniac's interest? The intensity of a maniac's interest, for instance, in doing something harmful, may be much greater than the poor man's interest in preventing him from doing it. Is the maniac's interest more valuable because of its greater intensity?

The weakness of Perry's doctrine lies in his three criteria for deciding what is better or worse. The criteria of intensity takes for granted that all interests are of the same nature and therefore comparable. But that is not the case. My interest in ethics and golf are two different types of interests; they differ qualitatively and not only in degrees of intensity. If the interests refer to different people of different cultural background, the qualitative difference is much greater, and the criteria of degree of intensity loses sense.

---

33. *Ibid.*, pp. 620-21.

Similar objects can be raised in regard to preference as a criterion. My preference for Aristotle over Plato and for Bach over Chopin is different from my preference of apples over pears, or vanilla ice cream over fudge sundae.

Inclusiveness takes a democratic approach to values, an area in which democracy does not apply, as it does not in science. The truth of a theory cannot be decided by voting, nor can we decide the value of a painting or the honesty of a person in that way either. But he states that "interest is added to interest in the same objects, and these objects derive augmented value from the summation of the interests taken in them."[34] Though he explains in a footnote that the terms 'add' and 'sum' "are not to be thought of as having any precise arithmetic or extensive significance," it is clear from the meaning of the criteria that number is what counts. If we apply the criteria to literature, best sellers will be better than *Hamlet*, since there are more people interested in them than in Shakespeare's work. The same may be said of intensity and preference. People seem to have a more intense interest in best sellers, and there is no doubt that they prefer them to *Hamlet*, since that is what they buy and read.

There are other points that are not satisfactory in Perry's interesting theory. My basic objection is that his interpretation of values and the three criteria that he proposes are not able to solve conflicts of interest. A value theory is almost worthless if it does not provide a way to

34. *Ibid.*, p. 645.

solve actual conflicts, either of interests or any other kind.[35] The world is full of conflicts among nations, groups, institutions, individuals. Even within ourselves we frequently discover conflicting drives. How could we decide between these inner and profound moral conflicts, like agreeing or refusing to be drafted to fight in Vietnam, if interest is the only criteria? What kind of interest? I do not, certainly, have any interest in killing people. Interest needs a qualifier to have any moral meaning, and value does not derive from interest but from what makes certain interests valuable.

5. Logical Empiricism and the New Forms of Subjectivism

Logical empiricism is a really new position in contemporary philosophy. Just because it is new does not mean that it is true. It is a sign of lack of cultural maturity to consider the most recent work published as closest to the truth. Progress in philosophy is very different from that in the sciences; it does not, obviously, progress by linear ascendency.

The novelty of this philosophical movement has been pointed out to warn the reader against any possible confusion. It is true that the thesis of logical empiricism may be considered as an expression of subjectivism—and

35. His attempt to find some criteria to solve conflicts is unsuccessful. See *General Theory*, pp. 652-58. He partially acknowledges it: "We seem forced to conclude, therefore, that the problem of the comparative magnitude of two conflicting interests of equal intensity is insoluble, and that it is impossible to judge that one of their objects is better or worse than the other. To the question 'Is it better absolutely, or objectively, that this interest should prosper at the expense of that, or that at the expense of this?' there is, strictly speaking, no answer. One alternative is better relatively to the first interest, another alternative to the second; neither can be judged to be better on the whole," pp. 654-55.

for this reason we include it in this chapter—but this subjectivism does not coincide with the earlier variety, and one gets to it by means which the earlier forms had not envisaged.

The usual point of departure for logical empiricism is the work of Ludwig Wittgenstein, *Tractatus Logico-philosophicus*, published for the first time in 1921, in the *Annalen der Naturphilosophie* of Ostwald. As is the case with all philosophical currents, precursors or antecedents can be found in early thought. In general, all philosophers who have adopted an antimetaphysical position could well appear on the list of precursors. In ancient times, it is the Sophists and the Epicureans who have been expressly singled out by representatives of logical empiricism; in the Middle Ages, it is the Nominalists, and for the modern period, Otto Neurath offers three lists for England, France and Germany respectively.[36]

Since logical empiricism has been interested in different problems, the antecedents vary in each case. On the other hand, one should not confuse antecedents with similar contemporary movements. Pragmatism, instrumentalism, operationalism, and the English analytic school, have many points of contact with logical empiricism, but are certainly not to be considered antecedents on that account.

Whatever the antecedents may be, it is correct to take the work of Wittgenstein as the conventional point of departure, since it is the first written expression of logical

---

36. Bacon, Hobbes, Locke, Hume, Bentham, J. S. Mill and Spencer in England; Descartes, Bayle, D'Alembert, Saint-Simon, Comte and Poincaré in France; Leibniz, Bolzano and Mach in Germany, Otto Neurath, *Le Développement du Cercle de Vienne et l'avenir de l'empirisme logique* (Paris: Hermann & Cie., 1935).

empiricism, and the one which spread some of its principal theses throughout the entire world.[37]

Nevertheless, the initial core of logical empiricism is to be found in the so-called Vienna Circle *(Wiener Kreis)* which was organized on the basis of a seminar, directed by Moritz Schlick in 1923. In 1925, the nucleus is definitely formed and the following year the movement acquires new impetus when Rudolf Carnap is invited to the University of Vienna. Carnap's work, *Der logische Aufbau der Welt* (Berlin, 1928), and particularly his theory of the composition of empirical concepts, as well as Wittgenstein's *Tractatus*, soon constitute the principal subject for discussion of the *Circle.*[38]

The work of this pioneer group acquires international significance when, in 1929, its program is published under the title, *Wissenschaftliche Weltauffassung: Der Wiener Kreis.* The unification of science *(Einheitswissenschaft)* constitutes one of the primary motives of the group. The procedure to be used in order to achieve the unification of the sciences, physical as well as social or cultural, including philosophy itself, was to be the logical method of analysis, such as had been initiated by Peano, Frege, Whitehead and Russell. This method would permit the elimination of metaphysical problems and all of those statements which were lacking in meaning, and would serve to clarify the

---

37. It should be remembered that a year after its appearance in the *Annalen*, the original German text was published in book form, together with its English translation (London: Routledge & Kegan Paul, 1922). The welcome which was accorded it by Russell and other distinguished representatives of British philosophy, assured the *Tractatus* considerable circulation.

38. On the beginning and development of logical empiricism, see H. Feigl, "Logical Empiricism," in *Twentieth Century Philosophy*, ed. by D. D. Runes (New York: Philosophical Library, 1947); Joergen Joergensen, *The Development of Logical Empiricism* (Chicago: The University of Chicago Press, 1951); and Otto Neurath, *Le Développement du Cercle de Vienne et l'avenir de l'empirisme logique* (Paris: Hermann & Cie., 1935).

concepts and propositions of the empirical sciences, by showing their immediately observable content *(das Gegebene)*.

Logical analysis, therefore, permits the determination of empirical propositions, reducing them to simple propositions which concern that which is given immediately and empirically. Besides the empirical propositions, there exist the so-called metaphysical propositions which are altogether lacking in meaning. These propositions do not affirm anything, nor can they, consequently, be said to be true or false. They are merely the expression of emotions; they belong, rather, to the realm of art, and are entirely lacking in cognitive content.[39]

This initial doctrine of the Vienna Circle was maintained in the subsequent development of logical empiricism, and was also applied to value theory.

The logical analysis of language led easily to the problem of meaning, and a vigorous new philosophic discipline arose by virtue of the efforts of the logical empiricists: semantics. The axiological problem would very soon be reduced to an examination of the meaning of such key terms as *good, beautiful, right.*

In fact, two men who bear no relationship to logical empiricism, had earlier arrived at conclusions similar to those of that movement. C. K. Ogden and I. A. Richards, in their book, written jointly in 1923, and entitled *The Meaning of Meaning,*[40] urged the necessity of analyzing the meaning of words and the relationship of language to thought. These men, who are not philosophers but

---

39. Cf. *Wissenschaftliche Weltauffassung*, pp. 16-17.

40. *The Meaning of Meaning: A Study of the Influence of Language upon Thought and of the Science of Symbolism* (London: Routledge & Kegan Paul, 1923).

linguistics and literary critics, pointed by means of semantic analysis to the existence of numerous philosophical pseudo-problems. Many of these problems arose out of the ambiguity of basic words in classic philosophy, such as "substance," "existence," etc.

There are two terms which traditionally represent the basic concepts of ethics and esthetics: good and beautiful. As these are two fundamental values, the analysis of these terms, made by Ogden and Richards, is important for value theory.

Let us look at the interpretation of the word "good." They write:

> This concept, it is said, is the subject-matter of ethics. This peculiar ethical use of the word 'good' is, we suggest, a purely emotive use. When so used the word stands for nothing whatever, and has no symbolic function. Thus, when we use it in the sentence '*This* is good', we merely refer to *this*, and the addition of 'is good' makes no difference whatsoever to our reference. When, on the other hand, we say '*This* is red', the addition of 'is red' to 'this' does symbolize an extension of our reference, namely to some other red thing. But 'is good' has no comparable *symbolic* function; it serves only as an emotive sign expressing our attitude to *this*.[41]

A similar attitude is adopted by various representatives of logical empiricism. These men believe simply that we do not assert anything when we use words which are basic both in our daily and philosophic vocabulary. We do not say anything about the object, act or person to whom we attribute the quality of being "good," but only express or evince our own emotions.

---

41. *The Meaning of Meaning* (3d ed., London: Routledge & Kegan Paul, 1930), p. 125.

This doctrine goes beyond subjectivism. We do not confer value upon an object by means of our pleasure, desire or interest as the subjectivists maintain; we only express our emotions when we say that something is "good" or someone is "honest."

This theory is not restricted to ethics; it also applies to esthetics as an analysis of the word *beauty* may show.[42]

In another book,[43] Richards advances a different axiological theory, one frankly subjectivist in orientation. "Something is valuable," he writes, "if it satisfies one's appetite, without implying the frustration of another, equally or more important."[44] Of course, it turns out to be very complicated for him to establish an adequate criterion for the determination of the degree of importance of an appetite.[45] On the other hand, the doctrine rests on a psychology which does not fulfill the requirements which he has imposed upon himself as a basis for his entire theory.

Charles L. Stevenson, perhaps because of the desire to eliminate the difficulties which are derived from the determination of the concept "important," interprets Richards' doctrine in a quantitative sense. He writes: "X is valuable" has the same meaning as "X satisfies more appetites than those which it frustrates."[46] The correction seems unacceptable, since the importance of an appetite, including its valuable character, does not always depend upon the quantity but on the quality or type of the appetite.

42. *The Meaning of Meaning*, pp. 146-47.

43. *Principles of Literary Criticism* (New York: Harcourt, Brace & Co., 1924).

44. Richards, *op cit.*, p. 48.

45. Cf. *ibid.*, p. 51.

46. Cf. his work, *Ethics and Language* (New Haven: Yale University Press, 1944), p. 9.

In any case, since appetites vary with the subject, the value nature of the objects will vary from one individual to another.

6. Rudolf Carnap

Rudolf Carnap (1891-1970) is the leading figure of logical empiricism, through his contributions, first in Europe, then in the United States, and his personal influence in the universities of Vienna, Prague, Chicago and California.

It is certainly not our purpose to examine Carnap's contribution to the development of logical empiricism or to undertake an examination of his diverse teachings. We will simply call attention to his principal works, before proceeding to the specific problem which interests us.

Carnap was called to the University of Vienna in 1926, when logical empiricism was taking its first steps, guided by Schlick.[47] Two years later, he published his important work, entitled *Der logische Aufbau der Welt (The Logical Construction of the World)*, in which he develops his theory of empirical construction of concepts, which gave great impetus to the Vienna Circle. His chief work, published in Europe, is the one that appeared in 1934, under the title *Logische Syntax der Sprache*, which two

---

47. He was a professor in Vienna (1926-1931), at the German University of Prague (1931-1935), and at the University of Chicago (1936-1954). When Hans Reichenbach died in 1953, Carnap was called to take his place at the University of California at Los Angeles, where he later became professor emeritus.

years later was published in English, with some additions, entitled *The Logical Syntax of Language.*[48]

The spread of Hitlerism in Europe forced Carnap, Reichenbach and other outstanding members of logical empiricism to abandon Europe and establish themselves in the United States, where they continued their research.[49]

Besides his teaching activities in different universities of the United States, Carnap contributed to the development of logical empiricism with various articles and five basic works: *Foundations of Logic and Mathematics* (1939); *Introduction to Semantics* (1942); *Formalization of Logic* (1943); *Meaning and Necessity* (1947); and *Logical Foundations of Probability* (1950). In the last twenty years his main interest was centered around induction and probability.

In his books *Logische Syntax der Sprache* and in *Philosophy and Logical Syntax*, Carnap examines the problem of ethics and formulates his interpretation of value.

For Carnap, judgments of value are disguised forms of norms or imperatives. There is no difference in content, but only one of formulation between the value judgment

48. A more simple exposition of the theory developed in this work is found in his book entitled *Die Aufgabe der Wissenschaftslogik*, published in 1934, the third volume in the series "Einheitswissenschaft"; and in his three lectures at the University of London, in October, 1934, which were published a year later under the name of *Philosophy and Logical Syntax*.

49. *The Journal of Unified Science*, under the guidance of Carnap and Reichenbach, continued the task begun in 1930 by the journal *Erkenntnis*. In 1938, two series of publications were started: one entitled *Library of Unified Science Series*, and the other under the title of *International Encyclopedia of Unified Science*. The Harvard Conference, held in 1939, and the contributions of the representatives of logical empiricism, attest to the continuity of the effort. A decade after Carnap's arrival in the United States, logical empiricism had penetrated North American thinking to such an extent that it was the most powerful philosophical current. A few years ago, its influence began to decline, and it later developed into analytic philosophy.

"it is bad to kill" and the imperative "thou shalt not kill."
The norm does not assert anything; it simply commands or
expresses a desire; the same is true of the corresponding
value judgment. In both cases, we are only expressing a
desire. The grammatical form of the value judgment is
what has deceived many who, believing that they were
dealing with a statement, sought arguments to prove its
truth or falsity. But value judgments do not affirm
anything and, consequently, cannot be true or false. In the
traditional language of logical empiricism, such a judgment
is not verifiable, and therefore is meaningless.[50] A
philosophical science such as value theory is not possible
since value judgments are neither true nor false, but
express instead a desire. Ethics and esthetics are dropped
along with value theory.

Carnap does not deny, according to his own words, the
possibility and the importance of a scientific investigation
of value judgments and acts of valuation. Because these are
acts of concrete individuals, they can be the object of
empirical investigation. Historians, psychologists and
sociologists can analyze and give explanations of such acts;
any study of this kind is empirical in nature, and is
therefore legitimate.

---

50. In a letter addressed to Ray Lepley, Carnap explains that he is referring to
cognitive meaning, and denies such meaning in the case of statements
concerning absolute values. He doesn't adopt a similar attitude when it is a
question of the probable consequences which certain acts might have. He
writes: "To call a kind of behavior good or bad is meant here as saying that it
is a suitable or unsuitable way to a certain aim. For instance, 'killing is evil'
may be meant as saying: 'killing is not a suitable way to further a harmonious
community life.' On the basis of any interpretation of this kind, e.g., in terms
of instrumental function or of human interests or the like, a value statement
has obviously factual, cognitive content. . . . " And he adds: "Since the word
'meaning' is often used in a wider sense, I wish to emphasize that the kind of
meaning which we deny for absolute value statements is only cognitive
(theoretical, assertive) meaning. These statements certainly have expressive,
especially emotive and motivative meaning; this fact is of great importance for
their social effectiveness." Cf. R. Lepley, *Verifiability of Value* (New York:
Columbia University Press, 1944), pp. 137-38, n. 14.

7. The Emotive Theory

A theory close to that of logical empiricism is that held by the English philosopher, Alfred J. Ayer, of Oxford University.[51] He agrees with logical empiricism in stating that so-called value judgments, and in particular, ethical and esthetic judgments, are neither true nor false because they do not assert anything, but rather express the sentiments of the person who makes the judgment.

Ayer's conception should not be confused with the ordinary subjectivist theory. The difference can be clearly shown if one points to the distinction made between *expressing* a feeling and *asserting* that one feels it.

The confusion between "asserting" and "expressing" a certain feeling arises because the assertion that one has a certain feeling often accompanies the expression of that feeling. Thus, for example, I can express that I am bored and assert that I am; my assertion may be taken as one of the ways of expressing my boredom. But I can express my boredom in several different ways without asserting it.

Ordinary subjectivism holds that he who makes a value judgment asserts the existence of a certain feeling such as his interest or approval of the value in question. In that case his judgment will be true or false, since it may or may not be true that he has the feelings which he asserts.

On the other hand, for Ayer, he who makes a value judgment is merely *expressing*, not asserting, a given feeling. And the expression of a feeling is neither true nor false, just as a burst of laughter or a scream of terror is not true or false.

---

51. Ayer made explicit his connection with logical positivism. He wrote in the Preface of his book *Language, Truth and Logic:* "The philosophers with whom I am in the closest agreement are those who compose the 'Viennese circle,' under the leadership of Moritz Schlick, and are commonly known as logical positivists. And of these I owe most to Rudolf Carnap."

When someone says "What a beautiful painting this is," he is not saying anything about the painting, as the objectivists maintain, nor about his feeling, as the subjectivists would think; he is simply expressing his feelings. He might just as well have shouted for joy or uttered an exclamation. Ayer rejects the subjectivist doctrine which holds that to call a thing "good" or an action "right" means that it is generally approved, for it is not contradictory to affirm that some actions which deserve general approval are not "right" or that there are things which are generally approved of which are not "good." For similar reasons, he rejects the strictly subjectivist doctrine—in opposition to the previous one, sociological—which holds that an individual's assertion that an act is right or that a thing is good, is equivalent to saying that he himself approves of it. In fact, says Ayer, the man who confessed that he approved of what is wrong, is not contradicting himself.[52]

According to ordinary subjectivist and objectivist doctrines, value judgments are true or false. Ayer disagrees and maintains that we cannot argue about axiological questions, for if a value judgment does not imply a proposition, axiological propositions cannot contradict each other. And he goes further: he asserts that we never argue about questions of value, but rather about questions of fact.[53] If we disagree with someone about the moral

52. Alfred J. Ayer, *Language, Truth and Logic* (London: Gollancz, and New York; Dover Publications, 1950) p. 104. His axiological doctrine is presented in the first part of Chapter VI. See also Introduction, pp. 20-22. The work was first published in January 1936, and in November of the same year, was in its third edition. In 1950, eleven editions had been printed, a testimony of the success of this book, as excellent as it is controversial. Later he modified his original thesis. See his article "On the Analysis of Moral Judgments," *Horizon*, Sept. 1949, pp. 171-84; reprinted in *Philosophical Essays* (London: 1954), pp. 231-49.

53. *Language, Truth and Logic*, p. 110.

value of a given action, it is evident that we use arguments to convince him that we are right. But we do not try, says Ayer, to show him that he has wrong ethical feelings, but rather that he is mistaken about the facts of the case. We may argue, for instance, that he is mistaken about the agent's motives; or that he has misjudged the effects of the action, or that he has not taken into consideration the special circumstances in which the person who committed the act found himself. Since the individual with whom we generally argue has had a moral education similar to ours, and lives in the same social order as we do, our efforts to convince him with factual reasons concerning an apparent axiological question are usually justified. But if our opponent does not agree with us in our axiological estimate—after being in complete agreement about the facts—because he has a different set of values, then we have to abandon the attempt to convince him by argument. We will argue that his set of values is wrong, or that ours is superior, but there will be no way of proving that this is really so, since such an assertion is a judgment of value and therefore outside the scope of argument.

Consequently, a discussion of moral problems is possible, only if both parties agree on a particular system of values. Any axiological discussion, especially of a moral nature, consists in showing the other disputant that the fact under consideration belongs to the class of acts which he either condemns or approves. In order to convince him, we shall have to examine the fact and see whether it really possesses the characteristics of acts which we approve or reject.[54]

According to Ayer, this is so because the so-called ethical concepts are pseudo-concepts and therefore cannot be analyzed. Hence, the presence of one of these words

54. *Ibid.*, p. 111.

does not add anything to the factual content of a proposition. For example, if I say to someone: "You acted wrongly in stealing that money," I am really asserting the same thing as if I said: "You stole that money." In saying that this action is wrong, I add absolutely nothing to the empirical content of the statement; I am only evincing my moral disapproval of it. It is as if I had said: "You stole that money" in a tone of horror.[55]

Now then, if I proceed from the concrete act to an assertion of a general nature and say: "stealing money is wrong," I have made a judgment which has no factual meaning and, consequently, cannot be true or false. It is as if I had said, "stealing money!" in a tone of voice which reflects my disapproval. There is nothing in it which is true or false, and a person who might have different feelings about stealing could disagree with me but he cannot contradict me, since neither of us is making a factual statement—not even about our own feelings.

If judgments which contain ethical terms, or values in general, lack real meaning because they are neither true nor false, since they do not assert anything, then the only thing which we can legitimately enquire is what reactions they provoke or what kind of feeling they express. Both belong to the field of psychology, not to ethics. In fact, ethics, as a branch of legitimate knowledge, cannot exist for Ayer. The supposed ethical problems are either meaningless or they belong to psychology and sociology.

55. *Ibid.*, p. 107. As we shall see, when we examine critically Ayer's thesis, he makes two errors. On the one hand, he does not admit any fact which might contradict his doctrine, because he is interested in the logical structure of his theory; on the other hand, he inadvertently admits elements which, according to his doctrine, are not empirical. The previous example shows us this second error. We can omit the adverb "wrongly" which modifies "to steal," because this term carries with it implicitly a value judgment; one cannot steal "rightly." The verb "to steal" is not merely descriptive, but is weighted with axiological meaning. If we replace it with "to take" or some other descriptive verb, the meaning of the statement which we wish to make is not complete if the adverb is missing.

There is, then, no way of determining the validity of any ethical system and, consequently, it is meaningless to ask whether it is true or false. We can only enquire what are the set of values, or the ethical principles of a given person or group of persons, and what causes them to have the system of values or the feelings that they actually have.[56]

What has been said about ethics can be equally applied to esthetics:[57] in fact, it can be extended to the entire realm of values. Ayer expressly denies the existence of a world of values, different from the world of facts. Or rather, he holds that so-called value judgments are empirical judgments, or that they are lacking in meaning because they are mere expressions of an emotional nature. This is the famous emotional theory of ethics and axiology of which Charles L. Stevenson is an enthusiastic proponent.

Charles L. Stevenson, of the University of Michigan, developed independently and almost simultaneously with Ayer, a theory which is similar though not identical to Ayer's doctrine.[58] In 1937, he published in *Mind* an article under the title of "The Emotive Meaning of Ethical Terms." While Ayer holds that ethical and axiological terms are purely emotive, Stevenson maintains that they are partly emotive and partly descriptive.[59]

56. *Ibid.*, pp. 103 and 113.

57. *Ibid.*, pp. 113-14.

58. For an antecedent of both doctrines, see W. H. F. Barnes, "A Suggestion About Value," *Analysis,* 1 (1933), reprinted in W. Sellars and J. Hospers, *Readings in Ethical Theory* (New York: Appleton-Century-Crofts, 1952), pp. 391-92. C. D. Broad anticipated in 1934 not only Ayer's ideas but also Stevenson's and Hare's in his critical paper on G. E. Moore: "Is 'Goodness' a Name of a Simple, Non-Natural Quality?" *Proceedings of the Aristotelian Society,* **34** (1934). See espec. pp. 250-51.

59. Cf. Ayer, *Language, Truth and Logic*, p. 108 and Stevenson, *Ethics and Language*, Chap. IX and pp. 210, 267 and *passim.*

On the other hand, he wants to stay away from merely descriptive theories of value, such as Perry's. In his article on "The Emotive Meaning of Ethical Terms" he says that:

> Traditional interest theories hold that ethical statements are *descriptive* of the existing state of interests—that they simply *give information* about interests. (More accurately, ethical judgments are said to describe what the state of interests is, was, or will be, or to indicate what the state of interests *would* be under specified circumstances.) It is this emphasis on description, on information, which leads to their incomplete relevance. Doubtless there is always *some* element of description in ethical judgments, but this is by no means all. Their major use is not to indicate facts but to *create an influence*. Instead of merely describing people's interests they *change* or *intensify* them. They *recommend* an interest in an object, rather than state that the interest already exists.[60]

In 1944 Stevenson published his now famous book on *Ethics and Language,* where he insists on his criticism of Perry, while acknowledging his indebtedness. He wrote: "By passing over agreement and disagreement in attitude, giving exclusive emphasis instead to agreement and disagreement in belief about attitudes, Perry makes normative ethics a direct branch of natural sciences, and so gives an illusory certitude to ethical methodology.[61]

---

60. *Facts and Values: Studies in Ethical Analysis* (New Haven: Yale University Press, 1963), p. 16. He presents in book form ten articles previously published, and a new essay.

61. *Ethics and Language,* p. 268. He devotes four pages (268-71) to his indebtedness to and disagreements with Perry. Perry's reaction to Stevenson's book may be inferred from his comment, in a footnote, that *Ethics and Language* should be "treated like a book on 'physics and language'—interesting, but not physics." *Realms of Value,* p. 8, n. 1. This is the only reference to Stevenson in the whole book.

Both Ayer and Stevenson hold that "ethical terms do not serve only to express feelings. They are calculated also to arouse feeling, and so to stimulate action."[62]

Besides the more technical and rigorous presentation of the doctrine, one of Stevenson's contributions to the emotive theory is his emphasis on attitudes. He proposes to replace *emotion* by *feeling* or *attitude*. For him, the term "feeling" designates an affective state that reveals its full nature to immediate introspection. He points out that an attitude is more complicated and a precise definition of it "is a matter too difficult to be attempted here." The term should "be understood from its current usage, and from the usage of the many terms ('desire', 'wish', 'disapproval', etc.) which name specific attitudes."[63]

Stevenson is less radical than Ayer in his philosophical analysis of ethical and axiological terms. Ayer's analysis dissolves normative ethics and value theory into psychological and sociological inquiries about the actual behavior of people. Stevenson, on the other hand, tries to clarify the meaning of the ethical terms, and to characterize the methods by which ethical judgments can be proved or supported. While he thinks that, as an analytic philosopher, he could not participate in the ethical inquiries, he does not deny the possibilities of such inquiries, but considers that "normative questions constitute by far the most important branch of ethics,"

---

62. Ayer, *Language, Truth and Logic*, p. 108. Cf. Stevenson, *Ethics and Language. Passim.* When he wrote *Ethics and Language*, in which he develops his ideas advanced in the article published in 1937, he acknowledged several of Ayer's contributions. Ayer, on the other hand, apologizes for not having had the opportunity to see Stevenson's article. For a comparison of both theories as seen by Stevenson, cf. his *Ethics and Language*, pp. 265-68.

63. *Ethics and Language*, p. 60.

and he adds: "The present volume has the limited task of sharpening the tools which others employ."[64]

Carnap's, Ayer's and Stevenson's theories are usually called *nondescriptive* or *noncognitive* because they hold that ethical judgments are not assertions.[65] The present nondescriptive theories have a tendency to be less radical. They admit the possibility of giving reasons to justify value judgments. Evaluating, as well as prescribing and commending is not an arbitrary act or mere expression of the speaker's feeling or attitude. There is, therefore, a place for reasons. An important problem arises from this new approach, namely, what kind of reasons are relevant to justify a value judgment.

But let us now examine Bertrand Russell's doctrine, so similar to Ayer's in many respects, and let us leave for Chapter V the critical appraisal of this, as well as the rest of the subjectivist doctrines.

8. Bertrand Russell

Bertrand Russell (1872-1969) was one of the most brilliant personalities in the contemporary philosophical world. Nothing was foreign to him; he has contributed ingenious and often fruitful theories to all fields. His major

---

64. *Op. cit.*, p. 1.

65. More attention has been paid to Ayer's theory than to any other, because it is the most radical one. The reader should know how far he can go in each direction if he wants to have a comprehensive picture of the whole situation.

contribution is to be sought in the strictly technical
disciplines, particularly in mathematical logic.[66] He has
always adopted a "scientific" approach to philosophy, and
this attitude has drawn him closer to logical empiricism. At
first, he distinguished himself by his concern with the basis
of mathematics and his contributions to symbolic logic,
but before long he undertook, with youthful enthusiasm,
to examine the major portion of the philosophic and social
problems of the age. His pacifism landed him in jail during
World War I, and kept him quite active even at the age of
97. His writings on divorce, sexual problems, international
relations and other thorny political and social topics of
this century, made him controversial and often unpopular
and he always reacted with subtle irony. He was one of the
most prolific philosophers and his clear and agile style
afforded him vast popularity. He published more than fifty
volumes and several hundred articles; by 1935, seventeen

66. As is well known, in 1903 he published *The Principles of Mathematics*,
and in 1910, the first volume of *Principia Mathematica*, written in
collaboration with Whitehead. The other two volumes were published in 1912
and 1913. The following may be considered his principal works. *An Essay on
the Foundations of Geometry* (1897); *A Critical Exposition of the Philosophy
of Leibniz* (1900); *The Principles of Mathematics* (1903); *Philosophical Essays*
(1910); *The Problems of Philosophy* (1912); *Our Knowledge of the External
World as a Field for Scientific Method in Philosophy* (1914); *Scientific
Method in Philosophy* (1914); *Principles of Social Reconstruction* (1916);
Political Ideals (1917); *Mysticism and Logic and Other Essays* (1918); *Roads
to Freedom: Socialism, Anarchism and Syndicalism* (1918); *Introduction to
Mathematical Philosophy* (1919); *The Analysis of Mind* (1921); *Free Thought
and Official Propaganda* (1922); *The ABC of Atoms* (1923); *Logical Atomism*
(1924); *The ABC of Relativity* (1925); *On Education Especially in Early
Childhood* (1926); *The Analysis of Matter* (1927); *An Outline of Philosophy*
(1927); *Sceptical Essays* (1928); *The Conquest of Happiness* (1930); *The
Scientific Outlook* (1931); *Education and the Social Order* (1932); *Freedom
and Organization 1814-1914* (1934); *Which Way to Peace?* (1936);
Determinism and Physics (1936); *An Inquiry into Meaning and Truth* (1940);
A History of Western Philosophy (1946); *Physics and Experience* (1946);
Human Knowledge (1948). A complete bibliography of Russell's writings until
1944 can be found in the volume edited by P. A. Schilpp, *The Philosophy of
Bertrand Russell* (Evanston: Northwestern University Press, 1944), now
published by the Open Court Publishing Co., La Salle, Illinois. Subsequent to
this date, Russell has published numerous articles and various works.

volumes were translated into German. There is not a civilized language that does not know at least one of Russell's books.

Besides his voluminous polemical writings, Russell produced first-class philosophical contributions. He is therefore appreciated equally by the general public as well as the specialist. His theory of values is set forth chiefly in a work, polemical and popular in tone—*Religion and Science*[67] which highlights the philosophical attitude that always distinguished him. His antireligious and antimetaphysical thought is joined in this work to a polemical attitude which in him is always a mixture of fine, sharp irony, and acid aggressiveness. A generous spirit, ever ready to correct his mistakes, individualist by temperament and conviction, he fought openly against totalitarianism and all institutions which represent the curtailment of man's liberty. As a great defender of religious tolerance, he always was a severe judge of religious organizations, particularly of clericalism.

This general characterization can help us not only to understand the man behind the doctrine which interests us, but also to capture the intimate meaning of his theory which is the result of a combination, frequently found in Russell, of a calm and objective scientific examination and an uncontrolled, polemic passion.

Russell holds that the questions of values lie outside the domain of science, not because they pertain to

67. *Religion and Science* (New York: Henry Holt, 1935) and Home University of Modern Knowledge (London: Butterworth-Nelson, 1935). He also discusses values in the following works: *The Elements of Ethics* (1910), *What I Believe* (1925), *An Outline of Philosophy* (1927), *Power* (1938), and *Human Society in Ethics and Politics* (1955). In 1944 he elaborated somewhat upon his ideas in his reply to J. Buchler, in the volume edited by P. A. Schilpp, *The Philosophy of Bertrand Russell*, pp. 719-25.

philosophy, but because "they lie wholly outside the domain of knowledge."[68] When we say that something has value, we do not state a fact independent of our personal feelings; we are instead "giving expression to our own emotions."[69]

In order to prove his thesis, he starts with an analysis of the idea of *good*. What he states with reference to good may be applied to other values. He claims that "it is obvious that the whole idea of good and bad has some connection with *desire*."[70] This connection between what is good and what is desired is the main hypothesis of his entire doctrine which he does not analyze critically at any time. For him, ethics is the attempt to give universal importance to certain personal desires.

Man does not perceive the connection between the good and the desired, according to Russell, because he does not grasp the sense of the words involved. Thus, when he says "this is good in itself," he thinks he is making a statement similar to "this is square" or "this is sweet." Whereas in the latter statements, an objective property of something is stated, in the first assertion only a desire is expressed. One might well replace this with another: "I wish everybody to desire this;" or rather, "Would that everybody desire this." In such a case, the truth or falsity of what has been said cannot be discussed, since only a desire has been expressed. If one wishes to interpret it as a statement, he will have to claim it as an assertion of his own wish.

68. *Religion and Science* (New York: Holt, Rinehart, and Winston, Inc.), p. 230. Russell had pointed out earlier the connection between goodness and desire. He wrote in *An Outline of Philosophy* that "we call something 'good' when we desire it" (p.242); and in *What I Believe*, that it is "our desires which confer value." (p. 17).

69. *Loc. cit.*

70. *Religion and Science*, p. 231.

What confuses people and serves as a basis for the supposedly objective nature of value, according to Russell, is that the wish is personal, but what it desires is universal. To clarify the issue, he compares a statement, supposedly ethical in content, with another one which may actually be so. If I say "All Chinese are Buddhists," I can be refuted by being shown a Chinese who is a Christian, for example. On the other hand, if I say "I believe that all Chinese are Buddhists," the refutation cannot be of the same kind; instead, it will have to be proved that I do not believe what I say. If someone asserts "Beauty is good," I can interpret this to mean "Would that everybody loved the beautiful;" (which corresponds to "All Chinese are Buddhists") or "I wish that everybody loved the beautiful" (which corresponds to "I believe that all Chinese are Buddhists"). The first sentence does not affirm anything; it merely expresses a wish. The second makes an assertion, but it is about the person's mind. It could be refuted by showing that he has not the wish he says he has. The first sentence, which belongs to ethics, has no cognitive content, since it expresses a desire, but asserts nothing.

Russell's doctrine coincides in this respect with Ayer's.[71] Both deny that there are ethical propositions, that is to say, sentences with cognitive content, and therefore they place ethics and axiology beyond the domain of "scientific" knowledge. But while Ayer expressly rejects subjectivism, Russell states that his theory

71. In fact, Russell anticipated Ayer. *Religion and Science* was published in 1935, while Ayer's work appeared in January, 1936. But Russell is not bothered about the priority of a theory. In this same chapter on "Science and Ethics," he observes in passing that "the philosopher may, it is true, sink to the level of the stock-jobber, as when he claims priority for a discovery. But this is a lapse; in his purely philosophic capacity, he wants only to enjoy the contemplation of Truth in doing which he in no way interferes with others who wish to do likewise." *Ibid.*, p. 233.

is "a form of the doctrine which is called the 'subjectivity' of values."[72] If two men disagree on values, says Russell, they are not disagreeing about the truth of anything but only about taste.

Up to this point, Russell has been rather dogmatic in the exposition of his viewpoint; he states what he thinks but he does not take much trouble in giving reasons; he seems to express his own wishes leaving the reader with a host of questions and objections at the tip of his tongue. At this point he offers the first reason: "The chief ground for adopting this view [the subjectivist doctrine of values] is the complete impossibility of finding any arguments to prove that this or that has intrinsic value."[73]

Let us postpone the critical examination of this and other aspects of Russell's thesis till the last chapter and see what consequences follow from his doctrine.

If every dispute over values implies a difference in taste, and there is no objective criterion to determine who is in the right, "sin" disappears. An act which is sinful for one man, writes Russell, can be virtuous for another. There is no binding agreement which one or the other may use to convince someone else who thinks differently that he is in error. "Hell, as a place of punishment for sinners, becomes quite irrational."[74]

The fact that this doctrine eliminates all forms of sin does not imply for Russell that it carries with it immoral consequences; much less does it mean a weakening of the sense of moral obligation. Moral obligation, in order to influence our conduct, should not consist in mere creed,

---

72. *Ibid.*, p. 237. Stevenson states that Russell and Ayer have an almost identical position with respect to this problem. Cf. *Ethics and Language* (New Haven: Yale University Press, 1953), p. 265.

73. *Religion and Science*, p. 238.

74. *Ibid.*, p. 239.

but in desire. Russell is right in making this assertion; what is not so clear is the question: What prevents that desire from being immoral? That is to say, what is the criterion which he uses to valuate a desire? "The sort of life that most of us admire," he writes, "is one which is guided by large impersonal desires."[75] Why should impersonal desires be superior to those which are fed by egoism? Inasmuch as they are desires, they have the same hierarchy; there is probably an axiological element which differentiates them. Like all extreme "scientists," Russell is forced to let something gain access through the window, which his doctrine prevented from coming in through the door. He wants—and rightly so—impersonal desires to be stimulated by example and through education, but he does not offer any reason in favor of impersonal desires or any criteria to distinguish a good from a bad desire. "The desire to be 'good' generally resolves itself into a desire to be approved, or alternately, to act so as to bring about certain general consequences which we desire."[76] The second alternative only postpones the question: How do we know that the consequences we desire will be good? The only criterion which is left is the sociological one: we want society to approve our behavior. What criterion will society use to approve or disapprove our behavior? If no ethical criterion exists, it will probably be judged by the desire which predominates in that society. And what if the society is corrupt? Will our desires be good when they win the approval of immorality? Russell's retort would probably be that there is no valid argument which determines whether a society is "corrupt" or "immoral"; the only thing we can say is that it has mores different from ours. If this is so, the immoral consequences of his

75. *Ibid.*, p. 240.

76. *Loc. cit.*

doctrine are self-evident. And if that is not his answer, he will have to admit some axiological element, over and beyond mere social approval, when judging a society from the moral point of view. We insist that Russell has a criterion by which to distinguish morally one individual from another, but since he is unable to put his criterion into the language of his philosophic theory, he uses it and at the same time maintains that it does not exist. The passage quoted above, concerning the "large impersonal desires" proves it; it is also confirmed by his statement that it is by means of "the cultivation of large and generous desires, through intelligence, happiness, and freedom from fear" that men can be brought to act for the "general happiness of mankind."[77] Why should we prefer impersonal, great and generous desires to those which are selfish, petty and mean? Is there or is there not a criterion to distinguish a good from a bad desire?

Russell's assertion can perhaps be admitted on a lower axiological level, that of pleasure and displeasure, and even in the political and legal spheres, but not on the ethical level. Pleasure depends on habit and conventional factors; the same thing happens, to a certain degree, in the political and legal fields; there are no forms of government which are good in and of themselves; their virtues depend on circumstantial, historical and cultural factors. The moral order is different: if one identifies what ought to be with what is, the good with the desired, then every criterion of morality is abandoned. Whatever happens is morally right or we should drop the word "moral" altogether.

The doctrine that we have discussed is Russell's best known theory, but he has changed his mind several times on this subject. When he first discussed this question he defended exactly the opposite doctrine. He wrote an essay

---

77. *Ibid.*, pp. 242-43.

under the title of "The Elements of Ethics," which was published in 1910,[78] and written under the influence of Moore's *Principia Ethica*, as he pointed out himself.[79] He there states that "*good* and *bad* are qualities which belong to objects independently of our opinion, just as much as *round* and *square* do; and when two people differ as to whether a thing is good, only one of them can be right, though it may be very hard to know which is right."[80]

He discusses the same question in *What I Believe* (1925); *An Outline of Philosophy* (1927); *Power* (1938) and particularly in the first part of his book *Human Society in Ethics and Politics* (1955). The hesitation in his doctrine shown his dissatisfaction with his own ideas on the matter. He wrote in 1952: "I am not, however, quite satisfied with any view of ethics that I have been able to arrive at, and that is why I have abstained from writing again on the subject."[81] But he *did* write about ethics after that, however, though not changing his position much.

It would be very difficult to cover all the different subjectivistic interpretations of values. We have picked up the most representative positions, particularly in the English-speaking world. The ideas of Carnap, the

---

78. This essay was included in Russell's *Philosophical Essays* (London: Longmans, Green and Co., Ltd., 1910). There is a revised edition (London: Allen Unwin, 1966); and it was reproduced in W. Sellars and J. Hospers, *Readings in Ethical Theory* (New York: Appleton-Century-Crofts, Inc., 1952), pp. 1-32.

79. Sellars and Hospers, *op. cit.*, p. 1.

80. Russell, *Philosophical Essays*, 1910 ed., p. 11; 1966 ed., p. 21. Sellars and Hospers, p. 7.

81. Sellars and Hospers, *op. cit.*, p.1.

emotivists and Russell have been channeled and enriched
in analytic philosophy which is at present very prolific.[82]
In continental Europe, several forms of subjectivism took
existentialism as a starting point, and particularly Sartre's
Being and Nothingness.[83]

82. From 1950 on, the following books deserve to be particularly mentioned:
S. E. Toulmin, *An Examination of the Place of Reason in Ethics* (1950);
R. M. Hare, *The Language of Morals* (1952);
P. H. Nowell-Smith, *Ethics* (1954);
K. Baier, *The Moral Point of View* (1958);
R. M. Hare, *Freedom and Reason* (1963);
C. Stevenson, *Facts and Values. Studies in Ethical Analysis* (1963);
G. H. von Wright, *The Varieties of Goodness* (1963);
G. H. von Wright, *Logic of Preference* (1963).

83. See, for instance, Raymond Polin's books and particularly *La création des valeurs* (Paris: Presses Universitaire de France, 1945).

9. Bibliography

AYER, Alfred J. *Language, Truth and Logic.* London: Gollancz, 1950. See Introduction and Chapter VI.

_____ . *Philosophical Essays.* London: Macmillan, 1963. See Essay 10.

CARNAP, Rudolf. *Philosophy and Logical Syntax.* London: Routledge & Kegan Paul, 1935. See Chap. I, Sec. 4.

EATON, Howard O. *The Austrian Philosophy of Value.* Norman: University of Oklahoma Press, 1930.

EHRENFELS, Christian von. *System der Werttheorie.* 2 vols. Leipzig: Reisland, 1897-1898.

HARE, R. M. *The Language of Morals.* Oxford: Clarendon Press, 1952.

MEINONG, Alexius. *Psychologische-ethische Untersuchungen zur Werttheorie.* Graz: Leuscher u. Lubensky, 1894.

MOORE, G. E. *Principia Ethica.* London: Cambridge University Press, 1903.

_____ . *Philosophical Studies.* 2d ed. London: Routledge & Kegan Paul, 1958. See essay on "The Conception of Intrinsic Value."

PERRY, R. B. *General Theory of Value.* Cambridge, Mass.: Harvard University Press, 1926.

_____ . *Realms of Value: A Critique of Human Civilization.* Cambridge, Mass.: Harvard University Press, 1954.

POLIN, Raymond. *La création des valeurs. Recherches sur le fondemont de l'objectivité axiologique.* Paris: Presses Universitaires de France, 1945.

RUSSELL, Bertrand. *Human Society in Ethics and Politics.* New York: Simon and Schuster, 1955. See Part I.

_____ . *Religion and Science*. New York: Henry Holt, 1935.

SCHLICK, Moritz. *Problems of Ethics*. New York: Prentice Hall, 1938.

STEVENSON, Charles L. *Ethics and Language*. New Haven: Yale University Press, 1945.

_____ . *Facts and Values*. New Haven: Yale University Press, 1963. Ten important essays previously published.

TOULMIN, Stephen E. *An Examination of the Place of Reason in Ethics*. London: Cambridge University Press, 1950.

WRIGHT, G. H. von. *The Logic of Preference*. Edinburgh: Edinburgh University Press, 1963.

_____ . *The Varieties of Goodness*. London: Routledge & Kegan Paul, 1963.

Scheler
And
Material
Apriorism

The contemporary objectivist theories arise as a reaction against the relativism implicit in the subjectivist interpretation and from the need for a stable morality. Meinong experienced within himself the change which German axiology would later have to undergo, a change which started with the crude equating of value with pleasure.

The errors of early subjectivism helped the emergence of extreme objectivist doctrines which assumed that these errors permitted them to adopt a completely opposite position. Since subjectivism started with experience, these doctrines ignored empirical evidence and preferred to adopt an a priori method which possesses the dual advantage of assuring us of the supposed objectivity we are looking for, and of offering us the certainty that experience will not contradict us. One must merely attend to the logical coherence and esthetic presentation of the system; the use of proper language will gain the emotional support of the reader.

Many did not believe it necessary to offer opposing arguments to subjectivism which they definitely considered refuted; they preferred to look down upon it, accusing of value-blindness those who did not share their ideas. There were also those, especially in Latin America, who *pretended* to see so as not to be accused of being blind.

Since it would be inadequate to give only a general theory of objectivism, arbitrarily compiled from the different doctrines, and since it would be tiresome to enumerate all the different objective theories, it seems advisable to limit this chapter to a statement of one theory which stands out from the rest by its prestige and popularity in Germany and in Spanish-speaking world. We refer to the theory of Max Scheler.

1. Personality of Max Scheler

Perhaps there is no other man in contemporary German philosophy who can be compared to Scheler, by virtue of the force of his ideas and the captivating style of his prose. In contrast to the cold, logical rigor of his teacher, Husserl, and the excessively systematic spirit of Nicolai Hartmann, Scheler has succeeded in infusing prose writing with the emotional vigor which inspires his theory. Scheler did not place his personality at the service of his ideas; the latter, rather followed the course which his overflowing passion dictated to them. Professor Bocheński said of him, "Endowed with an unusual personality, Scheler was also beyond doubt the most brilliant German thinker of his day." "He is certainly the most original figure in ethical studies during the first half of the twentieth century."[1] Remaining aloof from mathematics and natural sciences for reasons of temperament, he always felt himself drawn to the problems of man, to which he devoted his whole life. Death prevented him from dedicating his chief work to philosophical anthropology.

There are some philosophers whose doctrines result from the influence of previous thinkers. Others are drawn to the works of earlier philosophers after they have reached their own ideas. This is the case with Scheler. He had deep emotional affinity with St. Augustine, Pascal, Nietzsche and the "philosophers of life." But it is sheer accident, I believe, that Scheler's passion was channeled through phenomenology. Phenomenology is for him rather a way out to Kantian rationalism and British empiricism. Husserl had an intellectual approach to essences, while Scheler experiences life in its existential fulness.

---

1. M. Bocheński, *Contemporary European Philosophy* (Berkeley: University of California Press, 1956), p. 140.

His whole restless life shows it, and it becomes evident in his reaction to Bergson's philosophy which he evaluates as a "movement of profound confidence in immediate experience and in surrendering oneself and abandoning one's ego to intuition and to love for the world," and he adds that the basis for such an attitude "is not a will to dominate the world, but the joyous impulse of one's existence."[2] Hence, he had to distort the sense of phenomenology and appeal to an emotional intuition of which his master disapproved. From this grafting of the emotional upon the world of essences, stem both the grandeur and weakness of Scheler. Grandeur, because he broadened the meaning of the phenomenological movement; weakness, because he made use of an idea which is foreign to emotions and tried to bring the logic of the mind to the level of the heart.

Passion is the enemy of the systematic; hence, Scheler did not succeed, nor did he attempt, to build a system. In fact, his tempestuous life and thought underwent great changes; they cannot be placed within the traditional confines of philosophic thought.. In general, three periods are to be distinguished in Scheler's life. In his youth, he was a student and disciple of Rudolf Eucken, under whose influence he wrote his thesis at the University of Jena, entitled *Contributions to the Determination of the Relations between Logical and Ethical Principles,*[3] and a work which reveals his subsequent orientation, *The Transcendental Method and Psychological Method.*[4] Shortly after, he came in contact with Husserl's phenomenology, and by way of the latter, with Franz

2. Cf. *Vom Umsturz der Werte*, pp. 164-65.

3. *Beiträge zur Feststellung der Beziehungen zwischen den logischen und ethischen Prinzipien* (1899).

4. *Die transzendentale und die psychologische Methode* (1900).

Brentano. Under the influence of phenomenology, his own thinking matured. This period, which ended in 1922, was initiated with the appearance of the first volume of *Der Formalismus in der Ethik*, published in the first volume of the *Jahrbuch für Philosophie und phänomenologische Forschung*, which appeared in 1913 under the editorship of Husserl. To this period there belong a large number of essays which were compiled in two volumes: *Concerning the Revolution in Values*[5] and *On the Eternal in Man*,[6] and his principal work, already mentioned, *Der Formalismus in der Ethik und die materiale Wertethik.*[7] This book contains the essence of Scheler's axiology, since his ethics can be resolved into a theory of values.

In the last period of his life, from 1923 to 1928, Scheler experienced a profound change. He abandoned the theist and Christian conception, which had served as the basis for his axiology, in order to strike out along the path of a revolutionary theological conception, as yet not completely formulated, but which was suggested in bold

---

5. *Vom Umsturz der Werte* (1919).

6. *Vom Ewigen im Menschen* (1921).

7. *Formalism in Ethics and the Material Ethics of Value*. The first part appeared in Husserl's *Jahrbuch* in 1913, and the second in July, 1916.

strokes in the final pages of his last book, *The Place of Man in the Cosmos.*[8] Here he writes:

> We reject all these conceptions on philosophical grounds. We must do so for the simple reason that we deny the basic presupposition of theism: a spiritual, personal God omnipotent in his spirituality. For us the basic relationship between man and the Ground of Being consists in the fact that this Ground comprehends and realizes itself directly in man, who, both as spirit and as life, is but a partial mode of the eternal spirit and drive.
>
> This is an old idea which we find in Spinoza, Hegel and many other thinkers: the original Being becomes conscious of itself in man in the same act by which man sees himself grounded in this being. . . .
>
> Thus, according to this view, the birth of man and the birth of God are, from the outset, reciprocally dependent upon each other. Even as man cannot find his own determination without recognizing himself as a link in these two attributes of the highest Being and as dwelling within this Being itself, so this Being, too, cannot find its own determination without the cooperation of man. Spirit and drive, the two attributes of being, are not complete in themselves—quite aside from the incompleteness of their mutual interpenetration which is their goal. They also grow in themselves in the process of the history of the human spirit and in the evolution of life in the world.
>
> I have heard it said that it is not possible for man to endure the idea of an unfinished God, or a God in the process of becoming. My answer is that metaphysics is not an insurance policy for those who are weak and in need of protection.[9]

---

8. *Die Stellung des Menschen im Kosmos* (1928). It has been translated by Hans Meyerhoff as *Man's Place in Nature* (New York: the Noonday Press, 1962). We prefer to keep the term *cosmos*, since *nature* is, for Scheler, only a part of the *cosmos*.

9. Meyerhoff's translation, pp. 92-94.

In *The Place of Man in the Cosmos*, he advanced an important theory of man, which has had an enormous influence upon philosophical anthropology of the present century. Its further development was cut short by his sudden death in 1928,[10] when he was on the point of beginning his courses at the University of Frankfort-am-Main.[11] This radical transformation in his thinking was already foreshadowed in his work *The Forms of Knowledge and Society*.[12]

2. Scheler's Ethics

Scheler's ethics arise from the desire to continue Kantian ethics, while overcoming Kant's rationalist formalism.[13] There is not the slightest doubt that Scheler considers Kant's ethics to be of the highest type which modern philosophic genius has produced. He writes in the

10. He was born in Munich in 1874. For an excellent account of his life and works, see John R. Staude, *Max Scheler: An Intellectual Portrait* (New York: the Free Press, 1967).

11. Scheler was a professor at the Universities of Jena, Munich and Cologne; in Cologne, from 1919 until shortly before his death. The University of Frankfurt-am-Main had invited him, but he died before beginning his teaching.

12. *Die Wissenformen und die Gesellschaft* (1926). The other principal works of Scheler are the following: *Über Ressentiment und moralisches Werturteil* (1912); *Wesen und Formen der Sympathie* (1923); *Schriften zur Soziologie und Weltanschauungslehre: Moralia* (1923); II *Nation und Weltanschauung* (1923); III, 2. *Arbeits und Bevölkerungsprobleme* (1924).
Posthumous works: *Mensch und Geschichte* (1929); *Philosophische Weltanschauung* (1929). Concerning the unedited works of Scheler, see article by Maria Scheler, "Bericht über die Arbeit am philosophischen Nachlass M. Schelers," in *Zeitschrift für philosophische Forschung*,II, 4, 1947, pp. 597-602.

13. There is no translation nor any important comment in English on Scheler's ethics or value theory.

Preface to the first edition: "Kant's ethic, more than that of anyone else among modern philosophers, represents to date the *most perfect* that we possess."[14]And he adds that "it is likewise an assumption of the author to believe that Kant's ethics have, naturally, been criticized, corrected and successfully perfected here and there by philosophers who have followed him, but have not been affected in their essential foundations."[15] The "unqualified appreciation" which he has for Kant's work is evident even where his words of criticism are tinged with harshness. Farther on he calls him a "colossus of steel and bronze."[16]

Nevertheless, Kantian ethics had to be rescued from the just accusation of formalism. This does not mean, of course, that Scheler admits that any of the trends of post-Kantian material ethics have refuted Kant.[17] His theory repudiates earlier, material ethics which were empiricist ethics of goods and ends, and reaffirms the apriorist principle established by Kant. This principle is the point of departure in Scheler's thinking. He points out, however, that Kant made two mistakes. In the first place, he confused the a priori with the formal; in the second, he confused a priori with the rational. Scheler's ethics aims to correct these two errors by means of a material ethic of values and an emotive apriorism. Such is the synthesis of Scheler's ethical thinking.

Since Scheler's axiology results from a desire to continue and correct Kantian ethics, perhaps the best way to make it clear would be to project it against the background of Kant's ethics.

---

14. Max Scheler, *Der Formalismus in der Ethik und die materiale Wertethik,* (Bern: Francke-Verlag, 1954), p. 9.

15. *Ibid.*, p. 10.

16. *Ibid.*, p. 30.

17. *Ibid.*, p. 29.

Scheler begins with Kantian apriorism and believes that Kant refuted all kinds of material ethics, based on experience and inductive validity, and which consider pleasure and happiness the highest values.

Kant's error consisted in equating the a priori with the formal, and in thinking that all material ethics necessarily had to be ethics of goods and ends, and have inductive, empirical validity. Kant also assumed erroneously that all material ethics were heteronymous, hedonist, the ethics of success, which led to the mere legality of conduct, not to the morality based on the will, and which centered the basis of ethical valuation in man's instinctive egoism.

Scheler admits, of course, that Kant rejected all ethics of goods[18] and ends, but he confused goods with values. Goods are value objects; it is therefore erroneous to want to extract values from value objects or to consider both on the same footing. Since the world of goods, consists of things, it can be destroyed by the forces of nature or history, and if the moral value of our will depended upon goods, such destruction would affect it. On the other hand, value objects have empirical, inductive value, and any principle which rests on them is condemned to relativism. How could a universal and necessary principle be derived from a changing, unstable reality? If the ethics of goods were admitted, moral principles would lag behind historical evolution and it would be impossible, Scheler claims, to criticize the world of existent value objects in any given age, since ethics would be based on these same value objects.

Every ethical principle which seeks to establish an end[19] with respect to which the moral value of desire is

---

18. *Güter* may be translated as *goods* or *value object*.

19. Scheler understands *end (Ziel)* to be "any content whatsoever—content of thinking, stating, perceiving—which is given for the purpose of *being attained.*" *Ibid.*, pp. 52-53.

measured is also in error. Ends as such are never good or bad, independent of the values which are to be realized. Good or bad behavior can therefore not be measured by relating it to an end, since the concepts of good and bad cannot be extracted from the empirical contents of the ends. One of Kant's merits is that of having divested all ethics of ends and goods. His error, as already indicated, consists in thinking that all material ethics are necessarily ethics of goods and ends, and consequently, should be rejected because of their empirical content. This would be true, says Scheler, if the values were derived from the value objects instead of being independent of them. Such independence allows him to work out an axiological ethic which is material and a priori at the same time.

In order to provide a firm groundwork for this purpose, Scheler would have to show that values are independent both of value objects and ends. This was really the task he undertook.

3.   Goods, Ends and Values

Without examining too thoroughly the problem of the nature of values, Scheler compares them with colors in order to show that in both cases, they are qualities which exist independent of their respective carriers. I may talk about "red" as a pure color in the spectrum, without experiencing the need to conceive of it as the covering of a surface, but rather as an extensive *quale*.

In the same way, value which is contained in a carrier, and makes an object valuable, is independent of that carrier. According to Scheler, we do not apprehend values though a generalizing induction. In certain cases, one single object or act enables us to fully grasp the value contained

therein. On the other hand, the presence of the value
confers upon the valuable object the nature of being
valuable. In this way, we do not extract beauty from
beautiful things; instead, beauty is prior to them.

We shall later have the opportunity to examine
carefully the axiological realism of Scheler and his
rejection of nominalism contained in these assertions. Let
us now look at the relationship that exists between values
and ends.

As has already been pointed out, "end" for Scheler is
any content of thinking, acting, etc., which is to be
realized regardless of who or what is to attain it.[20] It is
important that this content belong to the area of
representational content, and that it be represented as
something to be attained. Value, on the other hand, is
devoid of any image. Furthermore, Scheler distinguishes
between ends and objectives. An objective is to be found
in the process of desiring and is not conditioned by any
representational act; instead, it is immanent in the
tendency itself.

> Nothing can ever become an end without first having been
> an objective. The end is based on the objective. Objectives can
> be given *without* ends, but ends can never be stated without
> objectives which antecede them. We cannot create an end out
> of nothingness, nor can we 'propose' one without a 'tendency
> toward something' which precedes it. [21]

Well then, values do not depend upon ends, nor can they
do without them; they are, rather, embedded within the
objectives of the tendency as groundwork. They
constitute, with good reason, the basis of the ends which,
as we shall see, depend upon the objectives.

20. *Ibid.*, p. 52.

21. *Ibid.*, p. 61.

Since only ends possess representational content, a material ethic of values will have to be a priori with respect to all the representational content of experience.

All experience concerning "good" and "bad" presupposes a basic as well as previous knowledge as to what "good" and "bad" consist of. Kant rejected all attempts to derive inductively the concept of the good or moral law, from experience alone—whether historical or psychological. In fact, which criterion could we use to choose certain given actions, and not others? There is no doubt that we ought to have an a priori concept of good and bad in order to be able to separate good from bad actions, and to ascend in this way, inductively, to the generic concept of "the good."

For Scheler, empiricism is not wrong, as Kant believed, because duty cannot be derived from experience, but rather because values cannot be deduced from reality, of which they are independent.

According to Kant, duty, awareness of ethical law, precedes value; on the other hand, Scheler maintains that value precedes duty and serves as a basis for moral law.

It should be pointed out in passing, that although Scheler places values before duty and moral law, he does not admit that the former have an empirical base. If they did, they would have to depend on goods and ends, and therefore the criticism which Kant levels at all empiricist ethics would apply here as well. Scheler's ethic is a material ethic of values, not empirical but a priori. His whole ethic is therefore based on an axiology; the validity of his ethics depends upon the validity of such axiology.

4. Nature of Value

Well then, what is value for Scheler? We have already seen that value is a quality which is independent of its carrier, it is an a priori quality. Its independence refers not only to objects which exist in the world—pictures, statues, human actions, etc.,—but also to our reactions to them. "Even though murder were never 'judged' to be evil, it still would continue being so. And although 'good' had never been so considered, it would nevertheless be good."[22] "It is a matter of complete indifference to the essence of values, in general, whether an ego 'has' values or 'experiences' them (. . .) Just as the existence of objects (for example, numbers) or nature does not assume an 'ego,' much less is one implied by the essence of values."[23]

Values as independent qualities do not vary with things. Just as the color blue does not turn red when a blue object is painted red, so similarly values remain unaffected by the changes undergone by the objects in which they are embodied. My friend's treachery, for example, does not alter the value of friendship. The independence of values implies their immutability; values do not change. Moreover, they are absolute; they are not conditioned by any act, regardless of its nature, be it historical, social, biological or purely individual. Only our knowledge of values is relative, not the values themselves.

Scheler rejects, one by one, the subjectivist axiological theories. The dilemmas involved in the contemporary manner of looking at the philosophical problem are so inadequate, he states, that if one does not admit the reduction of value to what ought to be, the norm or the

22. *Ibid.*, p. 67.

23. *Ibid.*, p. 280.

imperative, one ends up by believing that the value essence of an object depends upon the relationship which it bears to our pleasurable experiences.

He refuses to accept the idea, granted even by Kant, that man aims at pleasure. Not only does he reject the theory which attempts to equate value with pleasure, but also that which sees in value a causal relationship involving a pleasurable effect. For Scheler, as we have seen, value is not a relationship, such as equal, or different, but a quality, similar to red or blue. For the same reason, the experiences of value cannot be reduced to those of relationships. We usually distinguish, he writes, between the value "in itself" of an object, and that which it has "for us."

Nor does Scheler approve of the idea, already expressed by John Locke and partially accepted by Kant, that values, although not properties of things, could very well be forces, powers or dispositions inherent in objects and capable of causing the corresponding experiences in the subjects. If this theory were accurate, says Scheler, every experience of value ought to depend upon the effect caused by these forces, and the hierarchical relationships among values would then have to be derived from the magnitude of such forces or dispositions.

He discards this theory, formulated originally for secondary qualities, such as colors. "We would have to ask ourselves in vain, he writes, just where do these 'forces', 'powers' and 'dispositions' reside."[24] Nevertheless, the answer seems simple: they reside in the value objects. Of course, Scheler cannot admit that this is a question involving properties which reside in objects, since he has

24. *Ibid.*, p. 39.

already taken for granted the independence of value with respect to objects.

> We are familiar with cases in which the value of a thing is presented to us clearly and evidently, *without* being confronted by the *carriers* of that value. Thus, for example, an individual may be unpleasant and repulsive in our eyes, or else, pleasant and charming, without our being able to show just *what* that consists of.[25]

The independence of values with respect to their corresponding carriers is one of the hypotheses of Scheler's axiology. Let us point out, in passing, that this is a highly debatable hypothesis. Is not plastic beauty, perhaps contingent upon the material which is utilized? On the other hand, in the example which Scheler offers in the section quoted above, there appears to be a confusion between the value carrier and the awareness, which is not always clear, in the one who grasps the characteristics of the carrier.[26]

Upon examining the relationship between the values and psychic phenomena within which they appear, Scheler observes that from the actual fact that value is given us via a "sentimental perception of something," a thesis has been derived erroneously, to the effect that values exist only to the extent that they are, or may be felt or grasped. Scheler, at this point, makes use of the phenomenological doctrine of intentionality in order to overcome the subjectivist thesis.

As is well known, Husserl, basing himself on his master, Brentano, took notice of the fact that psychic phenomena have intentionality, i.e., they point to something that is outside of inner experience; in perception, one perceives

---

25. *Ibid.*, p. 40.

26. Thus, for example, the beauty of a statue can depend on the material with which it is made. Our inability to discover this fact, does not eradicate it.

"something"; in remembering, "something" is remembered; in love "something" or someone is loved. That is to say, the "object" is presented to us as something irreducible to our own experience. The same phenomenon occurs in sentimental perception which reveals to us the presence of value.

"The phenomenological fact," writes Scheler,

> is that precisely in the sentimental perception of a value there appears that very same value, as distinguished from its perception—all of which is valid in every possible case involving a sentimental perception—and consequently, the disappearance of sentimental perception does not eradicate the essence of value.[27]

Scheler's axiological objectivism is intimately linked with his absolutism. Hence, he rejects all "relativist" theories, beginning with those which hold that values have existence in relation to man and his psychic or psycho-physical make up. Scheler believes that this theory is absurd, since animals also experience values, such as, e.g., that which is pleasant.[28] It occurs to us that we might ask if they do not possess such values, precisely because they possess, just as does man, a definite psycho-physical constitution. Of course, Scheler wants to advance beyond this point: he wants to render the existence of values completely independent of their apprehension. For him "there are an infinite number of values which no one has as yet been able to grasp or feel."[29] This truth appears to him as a "basic intuition," although, of course, it is not shared by many other axiologists. How can I be sure that there are values which no one has apprehended? Neither

27. *Ibid.*, p. 259.

28. *Ibid.*, p. 280.

29. *Ibid.*, p. 283.

man nor humanity, according to Scheler, is essential to the apprehension of values.

In the same way, he rejects the dependence of values upon life. He maintains that if values were dependent upon life, this would exclude the possibility of being able to attribute some value to life itself, that is to say, life in and of itself would be a fact, indifferent to value.[30] This type of reasoning, of course, could not be applied to many vitalist axiological theories; for these, life is the supreme value, and anything has value to the degree to which it advances what is vital.

For reasons which are similar to the above, he also rejects the theory which affirms the historical relativity of values. Historicist relativism, according to Scheler, attempts to derive values from historical value objects considering them to be products of history, and consequently, subject to its vicissitudes. It commits this error because it has not taken account of the independent nature of values, and confuses the real changes which value objects and standards undergo with variation in values.[31]

Not only does Scheler reject axiological subjectivism, but he also tries to explain the reasons for this doctrine. He maintains that among the reasons which led to it "there stands out in the first place the fact that it is *more difficult* to know and judge objective values than any other objective content.[32] It is true that even in subjectivist teachings appearing subsequent to Scheler's studies, this argument has been utilized in favor of the subjectivity of values. As will be recalled, Russell states that he adheres to subjectivism in the face of the impossibility of finding

30. *Ibid.*, p. 289.

31. Cf. *op. cit.*, Sec. V, Chap. I, & VI; also, pp. 498-99.

32. *Ibid.*, p. 331.

arguments to prove that something possesses intrinsic value.[33]

For Scheler it is a "shocking fact" to find ethical scepticism more widespread than the theoretical variety; on searching out the causes for this condition, he thinks they are to be found in the fact that we possess a greater sensitivity and concern for discrepancies in ethical judgments than in those of a theoretical order. Since we seek social approval for our ethical appraisals, we are disturbed whenever we differ with others, and this disturbance points up the existence of difference. Scepticism, in turn, is a result of the disillusion we experience when we fail to find expected agreement. This disillusion is due to our weakness and inability to stand alone in the presence of moral problems. A feeling of inferiority and "the profound and secret experience of impotence" in realizing values, and the resultant feeling of depression—all this leads, according to Scheler—to a "kind of vengeful act," which amounts to asserting the subjectivity of values.

The desire for social approval, according to Scheler, is what caused Kant to deviate from the truth "to the point of wanting to convert the mere ability to generalize a rule of will into an instrument of moral rectitude."[34] It should be mentioned in passing that for Scheler a desire is good exclusively for one individual without its being able to be generalized, and "a moral intuition of *pure and absolute values* [. . .] should be limited to individuals."[35]

It would seem unnecessary to point out at this stage of the discussion, that Scheler flatly rejects axiological

33. Cf. B. Russell, *Religion and Science*, p. 238.

34. *Der Formalismus*, p. 332.

35. *Loc. cit.*, cf. pp. 337-38.

nominalism which denies meaningful content to words
that express values: good, beautiful, honest, etc. Such
words are for nominalism expressions of feeling, interests
and desires of individuals, Scheler relates this theory to
Hobbes and Nietzsche; the reader will recall that
axiological nominalism acquires major significance
following Scheler's death, in various representatives of
logical empiricism and analytic philosophy.

Scheler asserts, and rightly so, that the arguments of
ethical nominalism are not any different, essentially, from
those which nominalist philosophy made use of in order to
deny objective validity and reality of concepts. And since
he considers Husserl to have demonstrated in his *Logical
Investigations*[36] the lack of a foundation in nominalism,
he does not feel the need to do it again.

Scheler thinks that a value cannot be reduced to the
expression of a feeling, because we frequently apprehend
values, independent of the feeling we experience. Thus, we
can grasp the existence of a moral value in our enemy.[37]
Nominalism does not succeed in explaining real human
behavior when faced with moral or esthetic actions; as a
matter of fact, he says, we act with respect to values in the
same way that we behave in the presence of colors and
sound, i.e., when we recognize their objectivity and
distinguish these qualities from their apprehension and the
interest we may have in them.

Scheler believes he has found something in common
between ethical nominalism and Platonism (which would
appear to be its opposite) and which he also rejects. "In
both conceptions 'independent acts of value' are denied

---

36. *Logische Untersuchungen*, second investigation.

37. *Der Formalismus*, Sec. IV, Chap. I, especially p. 189.

. . . the whole realm of morality" being relegated "to the sphere of a conceptual, rather than intuitive realm."[38]

Contrary to what Hartmann was to advocate later, Scheler does not believe that values should be sought for in the realm of ideal objects, together with numbers and geometric figures. It is true that the *concepts* of kindness, beauty, pleasure, etc., belong to that realm, but the moral—and with it, the axiological—are not restricted to the area of ideal meanings. Plato committed the error of placing values in this area because he started out with a fallacious division of the spirit, namely "reason" and "sensibility." Since values cannot be reduced to units of sensation, he grouped them together with numbers and geometric figures, i.e., in the realm of reason.

For Scheler, a distinction must be made between the concept of a value and the value itself. A six months old child experiences his mother's kindness before being able to have a concept in his mind of what is good. On the other hand, Plato denied the existence of negative values, considering the bad to be only apparent, in the face of the full reality of the good.

5. Apprehension of Values

The disagreement between Scheler and Plato is not so noticeable in the criticism which he makes,[39] but rather in the comparison between the methods of apprehension of values, of each philosopher.

38. *Ibid.*, p. 184.

39. *Op. cit.*, IV, 1.

Plato is a rationalist, opposed to the sensualism of the Cyrenaic school. Scheler, on the other hand, opposes all forms of rationalism and follows the line laid down by St. Augustine and Pascal.

He thinks that the rationalism of Plato and the great modern philosophers, including Kant, is based on the false division of the soul, indicated above. They chose reason because they reject sensibility; they do not realize that there is a third area, as dignified as that of reason, although equally independent of reason and sensibility. It is the *ordre du coeur* of which Pascal spoke. It is an order which is neither chaotic nor capricious, but which reason cannot succeed in grasping: "the heart has its reasons which reason does not understand." The light of emotion is extinguished when an attempt is made to transmit it to the intellect. Apprehension must be adjusted to the nature of the object apprehended. How, then, are values apprehended?

Values are a type of object, completely inaccessible to reason. Greek, as well as modern rationalism, relegated them to an inferior plane, or tried to merge them with entities of reason. They fit best the *logique du coeur* which has nothing to do with the logic of the intellect, but which establishes hierarchies and laws, as precise as those of the latter type of logic. Or, to put it in terms which are strictly Schelerian, values are revealed to us through emotional intuition, in preference, love, hate.[40]

In order to show the profound meaning of the apprehension of values by means of sentimental perception, Scheler undertakes a phenomenological description of emotional life, which makes it possible for him to reveal various levels in the realm of the emotional which are not usually distinguished very clearly.

40. *Op. cit.*, p. 339.

In the first place, he makes a distinction between "intentional feeling" *(intentionales Fühlen)* and "sensitive feeling state" *(Gefühlszustand)*. The latter refers to the pure experience as lived, whereas the former has to do with the apprehension of experience. In the affective or feeling state there is no intentional element; when an object is referred to, the reference is mediate, i.e., subsequent to the moment in which the feeling is manifested. The reference may be of a causal nature; thus, fire is the object which has caused the pain I have. The relationship is established by means of thinking.

On the other hand, in intentional feeling, there is a direct and immediate reference to the object, and this reference is not of an intellectual nature; in it, values are revealed to us. Sentimental perception is not joined to the object outwardly, or by means of an image; nor does the object appear as a sign of something which is hidden behind it.

We grasp values by means of the emotional experiences of sentimental perception. The hierarchical order of values is, in turn, expressed by "preferring" or "deferring" as we shall see farther on. Nor should we confuse "preference" with "choice." One chooses between actions, between one "doing" and another "doing," says Scheler, whereas we prefer one value object to another, and also a given value to another, regardless of the value carriers.[41]

Love and hatred, for Scheler, constitute the upper stratum of intentional emotional life. It is not a question of "states," since both possess a clearly intentional character. Language reveals this: one says "I love and hate 'something,' I do not just love and hate 'for the sake of' or 'in and of' something." Love and hatred have nothing to do with rage, anger, fury or any other similar experience.

---

41. *Ibid.*, p. 274; cf. also p. 107.

Nor should love and hate be confused with preference and avoidance. Preference requires a plurality of values, while in love and hate only *a single* value is involved.[42] Love and hatred are, in addition, spontaneous acts, very unlike thought-out reactions, such as vengeance, for example. They are acts in which the realm of values, accessible upon sentimental perception, undergoes an enlargement or restriction, since love is an authentic discoverer of values. Therefore, it does not lag behind sentimental perception and preference, but instead, precedes them, since it discovers new values for them.

Except for the few exceptions already mentioned, such as St. Augustine and Pascal, the history of modern philosophy reveals scant appreciation of the nature of emotional life and of its capacity to uncover for us a world of values.

Scheler distinguishes two periods in modern philosophy: the first, from Descartes to the end of the 18th century, and the second, from Kant onward. For the rationalist, Descartes, Spinoza, Leibniz, and the men who came under their influence, sentimental perception, loving, hating, etc., were not something irreducible, but rather confused and unclear aspects of thinking and understanding. For example, for Leibniz, maternal love is the confused concept that it is good to love one's child. And since they reduced emotional life to an inferior level of thought, good, evil and other values were reduced to degrees of perfection of being.

On the other hand, since the beginning of the 19th century, the irreducibility of affective life has been increasingly recognized, but the influence of the earlier rationalism caused Kant and the philosophers who follow him to downgrade emotional life, reducing it to simple states and consequently denying its intentional character.

42. *Ibid.*, p. 275; and *Wesen und Formen der Sympathie*, B.

In Scheler's view, by contrast, emotional life and sentimental perception, are irreducible to reason and possess an intentional nature. The fact that the essence of values is revealed to us in emotional intuition, and not in intellectual intuition, for example, shows plainly a basic characteristic which prevents its reduction to the world of ideal objects.

6. Hierarchy of Values

An essential characteristic of values is their appearance in hierarchical order though it is not easy to point out the criteria to use to find out such hierarchy. Scheler rules out the empirical criteria because it would only be able to determine the hierarchical table of a person, a society or an epoch, but could not tell us what this table *ought* to be.

Scheler believes that values are arranged in an a priori hierarchical relationship. The hierarchy for him is to be found in the essence itself of the value; it is even applied to those values which we do not know.[43] The superiority of one value over another is apprehended by means of "preference," which is a special act of cognition. To prefer is not to judge; axiological judgment rests on a preference which precedes it.

As has been pointed out above, one should not confuse "preference" with "choice." "Choice" is a tendency which already implies knowledge of the superiority of the value. "Preferring," on the other hand, is realized without exhibiting tendencies, choice or desire. When we say "I prefer the rose to the carnation," we are not thinking of a choice. Choice takes place in a field of action, as we have

43. *Ibid.*, p. 107.

seen. By contrast, preferring refers to value objects and values; in the first case, it is a question of empirical preference, and in the second, aprioristic.

Although the superiority of a value is not made evident to us before preference, but in the act of preferring, it should not be thought that this superiority consists in the mere fact that a value has, in fact, been preferred. Otherwise, superiority would have an empirical basis, while the hierarchy for Scheler is something inherent in the very essence of values, and therefore invariable and foreign to human experience. The hierarchical connection is of an a priori nature. This does not mean, however, that the hierarchical arrangement of values can be deduced logically; this is a matter of intuitive evidence of preference for which no logical deduction can be substituted.

The act of preference does not require a multitude of values to be present in the sentimental perception. An action may present itself to us as being preferable to any other action, without our thinking about or conceiving of the other possible actions; one's consciousness suffices for the purpose of being able to prefer any other thing.

Scheler differentiates between preferring as an action and the manner of its realization. At times, preference takes place intuitively, without our being conscious of any activity. On other occasions, preference happens to be conscious and is accompanied by "reflection."

Moral personalities depend upon the type of preferences. Some are designated by Scheler as being "critical" or "ascetic," since they realize the superiority of values, chiefly by way of deferring. These are offset by "positive personalities," for whom the inferior value becomes evident from the viewpoint of the superior which is given directly.

Although in preferring, the superiority of one value over another is already given, Scheler believes it necessary, and rightly so, to expound separately each criterion to be utilized in the determination of the axiological hierarchy. These criteria, five in all, can be separated from the acts[44] of preference. The first criterion is that of *duration (Dauer)*. Scheler observes that lasting value objects have always been preferred to those which are temporary and changeable. The ability to endure in the course of time is a sign which has characterized the great literary works, for example. Of course, endurance should not refer to goods, much less to the value carriers. A match can destroy a work of art, and a bullet can put out the light of a genius. The simple endurance of the value object through the strength of the carrier does not add value to the object. Otherwise an "ugly" statue of marble would be superior, esthetically, to a "beautiful" creation in wood or plaster.

Duration refers, undoubtedly, to values. Scheler asserts that "the most inferior values of all are, at the same time, values which are basically 'evanescent'; the values superior to all others are, at the same time, eternal values."[45] What is pleasant to the senses appears "essentially" as a transient value in comparison to the value of health, for example, or the value of knowledge.

The second criterion is that of *divisibility (Teilbarkeit)*. The height which values achieve is in inverse ratio to their capacity of being divided. We have to divide low values in order to enjoy them. Higher values resist division and one can enjoy them without any need of dividing them. Because values involved in what is sensibly pleasant "are essentially and *clearly* extensive," it is possible to enjoy them only by dividing them, as is the case with meals, drinks or a piece of fabric. In these cases, the quantity of the value is governed by the size of the carrier; a piece of

44. Cf. *ibid.*, pp. 110-20.

45. *Ibid.*, p. 113.

cloth or bread is worth approximately twice that of a half
piece. In a work of art, this does not occur; half of a statue
or a painting does not correspond to half of its total value.
For this reason, we can share the enjoyment of esthetic
values without having to divide the value objects (it is a
matter of complete indifference to spiritual values as to
how many people enjoy them). Therefore, material goods
separate people, conflicts of interest come into being,
because goods have to be possessed, whereas spiritual value
objects unite people because we may share them with other
people.

Foundation (Fundierung) is the third criterion. If one
value is the foundation of another, it is higher than this
other. It can be said that a value in class B is basic to a
value in class A, when individual value A, in order to exist
requires the prior existence of a B value. Value B, in this
case, is the value which furnishes the foundation, and is
therefore the higher of the two.[46]

Of course, all values are based on supreme values, which
for Scheler are religious values. In upholding this thesis,
Scheler is returning to an axiological monism, similar to
the medieval variety, which the development of modern
culture seems to have overcome.

The *depth of satisfaction (Tiefe der Befriedigung)* is the
fourth criterion. For Scheler there is an essential
relationship between the depth of satisfaction which
accompanies the sentimental perception of values and their
hierarchy. However, as in the case of preference, the
hierarchy of the value does not consist in the depth of
satisfaction which it produces. There is also, similarly, a

---

46. *Ibid.*, p. 114. If we accept this definition, there is, of course, no room for
discussion. The problem consists in knowing whether values in a given
area—e.g., esthetic—cannot be manifest without the corresponding
"grounding" values, religious values, for example. See my critical observations
on pp. 137-143.

"connection of essences" by which the highest value produces a more deep satisfaction.

Scheler clarifies the concept of "satisfaction." In the first place, it should not be confused with pleasure, although the latter may be a result of satisfaction. Secondly, it is a question of the fulfillment of an experience, i.e., it appears only when an intention is realized with respect to a value by virtue of the appearance of the latter. Satisfaction is not necessarily linked to a tendency; the purest case of satisfaction occurs in calm sentimental perception and in the possession of a positively valuable object. Nor is it necessary for satisfaction to be preceded by a tendency.

In the same way he clears up the concept of "depth." In the first place, he distinguishes it from "degree" of satisfaction.

> We say that a satisfaction derived from the sentimental perception of a value is deeper than another, when its existence appears *independent* of the sentimental perception of the other value, and of the 'satisfaction' attached thereunto, the latter, however, being dependent upon the former. [47]

Hence, it follows that only when we are satisfied at the deepest levels of our life, do we enjoy the naive, superficial pleasures.

Scheler recognizes that the four criteria enumerated—duration, divisibility, foundation and depth of satisfaction—"cannot express the last word with respect to the height of a value, however much they may rest on connection of essences."[48]

47. *Ibid.*, p. 116.

48. *Ibid.*, p. 117.

Let us see what happens in the case of the fifth criterion proposed: *relativity (Relativität)*. Scheler states that although objectivity pertains to all values, and their connections of essences are independent both of reality and of the actual connection with the goods in which the values are realized, there exists among the latter a difference which consists of a scale of relativity. He notes that the fact that a value is "relative" does not make it "subjective." A bodily object which appears as an hallucination is "relative" to the individual, but it is not subjective in the sense in which a feeling is subjective.

The value of what is pleasant is "relative" to a human being endowed with a sensitive feeling; on the other hand, those values are "absolute" which exist for the purpose of pure emotion—preferring, loving—that is, for an emotion independent of the essence of sensibility and of the essence of life. Moral values belong to this last category.

Relativity refers to the essence of the values themselves, and should not be confused with the dependence or relativity which derives from the nature of the eventual value carrier. The latter is a "second class" relativity, as opposed to the "first class" relativity which refers to values.

Those values found in feeling and preferring, which are shown to be closest to absolute value, appear in their turn as the highest in immediate intuition. Scheler believes that there exists an immediate perception of the relativity of a value, completely independent of judgment and reflection. Thus, absolute value is evident, regardless of any logical reasoning or empirical fact. In fact, reflection and acts of comparison and induction may hide from us the absolute or relative nature of a value.

> There exists within us a capacity whereby we appreciate secretly the nature of the values experienced by us, as concerns their 'relativity', notwithstanding the fact that we

may at times try 'to hide' that relativity from ourselves, by means of judgment, comparison and induction.[49]

The less relative a value, the higher it is: the highest value of all is absolute value. All the other connections of essences are based on the latter which is basic for Scheler.

Preference and the application of the five criteria indicated, reveal to us the following hierarchy or table of values.[50]

On the lowest level there are the values of sensible feeling, pleasant and unpleasant. In the second place, there are the values of vital feeling which are independent and irreducible to the pleasant and unpleasant. The noble-vulgar antithesis is fundamental in this axiological stratum although the values of well-being correspond to this area, and as states, all the modes of vital feeling, such as health, exhaustion, sickness, old age, death.

Spiritual values *(Geistige Werte)* constitutes the third axiological group. In the presence of these, vital as well as pleasure values should be sacrificed. We grasp these values via "spiritual" sentimental perception, and in such actions as spiritual preference, love and hate, which should not be confused with the corresponding vital acts of the same name.

Within the spiritual values, the following can be distinguished hierarchically: (a) the values of the beautiful and the ugly, and the other purely esthetic values; (b) the values of the just and the unjust, which are not to be confused with "right" and "wrong," as these refer to an order established by law, and which are independent of the idea of the State and of any positive legislation; (c) the values of "pure knowledge of truth," which philosophy

49. *Ibid.*, p. 119.

50. *Ibid.*, pp. 125-30.

attempts to realize, as opposed to positive science which aspires to knowledge for the purpose of controlling events.

It should be noted that Scheler speaks of the value of "knowledge" and not of truth itself; for him "truth does not belong to the universe of values."[51] Values of science as well as those of culture are "values by reference" to those of knowledge.

Over and above the spiritual values lies the last group of values, that of the holy and the unholy. Religious values cannot be reduced to the spiritual, and possess the peculiarity of being revealed to us in objects which are presented to us as absolutes. Scheler does not include moral values because they are the result of one's realization of higher values when confronted with lower ones.

Since values in general are independent of value objects of historical events, it can be understood that Scheler may claim for religious values complete independence from that which has all along been considered holy in the course of history, including of course "the purest concept of God."

Religious values are realized in ecstasy and desperation, which measure the proximity to or distance from the holy. The specific corresponding reactions are those of faith, worship and adoration. Love, in turn, is the action whereby we grasp the value of holiness.

For Scheler, this hierarchical relation of values which proceeds from the pleasant to the holy, is aprioristic and therefore precedes any relationship that may actually exist. It is applicable to value objects simply because it is applied to the values which are embodied in such objects.

We shall examine critically, in the fifth chapter, the validity of this hierarchy, and the criteria used to establish

51. *Ibid.*, p. 128, n. 2.

it. Suffice it for the moment to point out that every historical period and every great philosopher has had a table of values, and how difficult it would be to erect a definitive one, as Scheler claims to do.

7. Bibliography

BJELKE, Johan Frederik. *Zur Begründung der Werterkenntniss.* Oslo-Bergen: Universitetsforlagen, 1962.

BRIGHTMAN, E. Sh. *Nature and Values.* New York: Abingdon Press, 1945.

DUPUY, Maurice. *La philosophie de Max Scheler. Son évolution et son unité.* 2 vols. Paris: Presses Universitaires de France, 1959. See Part VI.

HARTMANN, Nicolai. *Ethik.* Berlin: Walter de Gruyter, 1926. English translation. London: Allen and Unwin, 1932. See Vol. I, Secs. V-VI; Vol. II. (Vol. III is devoted to "Moral Freedom.")

MALIANDI, Ricardo. *Wertobjektivität und Realitätserfahrung.* Bonn: Bouvier u. Co. Verlag, 1966. See Chaps. II and VI.

SCHELER, Max. *Der Formalismus in der Ethik und die materiale Wertethik.* Bern: Francke Verlag, 1954.

STAUDE, John R. *Max Scheler: An Intellectual Portrait.* New York: The Free Press, 1967.

URBAN, W. M. *Valuation: Its Nature and Laws.* London: Macmillan, 1909.

Value
And
Situation

1. Mistakes of Subjectivism

In spite of the emphatic assertions made by axiological objectivism and the certainty which the subjectivist thesis seems to offer, the problem of the nature of value is still open. It cannot be solved if one persists in adhering to either one or the other position, or if one pays more attention to logical coherence than to empirical evidence.

The difficulty originates in the complexity of the problem, and the fact that both doctrines make statements which are partially true. Both positions err in only considering one aspect of the problem.

Subjectivism is right in asserting that value cannot be entirely divorced from valuation, but it errs when it tries to reduce value to valuation. If values were nothing more than a projection of the pleasure, desire or interest of the subject, there would be axiological chaos, since desires and interests vary from one country to another and from one individual to another. And it is true that complete agreement does not exist; yet it is no less true that agreement is much greater than disagreement.

On the other hand, if values were created by the subject, without taking into consideration any element which might transcend the subject himself, the behavior norm would be reduced to personal caprice, and all possibility of establishing any stable form of esthetic appreciation would disappear. The table of values would fluctuate capriciously, ethical and esthetic education would be impossible, "good taste" and moral education would not make sense, and there would be no difference between the corrupt and the honest person; both would behave in accord with their own desires and the interests which motivate them.

If desire, pleasure and interest confer value upon an object, there could not be any erroneous valuation; the

mere act of desiring would suffice. To the psychological
act of valuation, certainly very important, it is necessary to
add the axiological element in order to know whether
what we desire is in fact worthy of being desired.
Subjectivism is not enough. Its contribution consists in
pointing out an important element in the axiological
relation, namely, the subject who evaluates, but it falls
short when it leaves aside, unconsciously or deliberately,
the other aspect of the relation.

Those who ignore the axiological aspect and believe
that knowledge refers only to questions of fact, do so for
methodological reasons and without considering the
peculiar nature of value. Generally, those who adopt this
attitude are philosophers inspired by the natural sciences
who wish to apply the criteria of this field to all other
areas, ignoring the differences. They are chiefly concerned
with the problem of method. These methods have proved
so successful in science, that they decided to apply them in
philosophy.

We think that the methodological problem is very
important, but the question of the nature of values is even
more important. Method is an instrument for discovering
the nature of reality. The problem of reality cannot be
replaced by methodology without committing the same
error as the individual who was told to observe through a
keyhole what was going on inside a room, and faced with
some difficulties, decided to describe the keyhole instead.

The fact that an acceptable criterion has not yet been
discovered for solving axiological conflicts, or for
determining the actual nature of value, does not mean that
such a criterion does not exist. It was a long time before
effective criteria were found for solving the problem in
science, and a premature desperate urgency would have
pushed the scientists into the field of magic, and scientific
procedures would not have been discovered. Axiology is a
very young discipline, and its problems are at least as

complex as the scientific, if not more so. In the face of failures to establish an acceptable criterion, we should not despair, still less should we arrive at the pessimistic conclusion that it is impossible to find such a criterion.

Once logical empiricists are convinced that there is no criterion with which to determine the nature of a value or its hierarchy, they conclude that value does not have a nature other than that which we project upon it.

Even if it did not exist, or if we were unable to find validating criteria, it would not be legitimate to infer, because of a methodological difficulty, the existence of certain qualities within the object under consideration.

Logical empiricists (and those, like Bertrand Russell, who are very close to this movement) have insisted more strongly in denying the existence of qualities which are characteristic of value, because there are methodological difficulties. As will be remembered, Russell asserts that his chief reason for adopting the doctrine of the subjectivity of value "is the complete impossibility of finding any arguments to prove that this or that has intrinsic value."[1]

Semantic analysis led the logical empiricists to similar conclusions. Carnap holds, as we have seen, that value judgments differ from expressions of desire and imperatives, only in their formulation. He then concludes decisively that normative ethics and axiology cannot be philosophic disciplines. These conclusions could be valid if one would first prove the thesis which underlies them—which Carnap does not do. Actually, it is not enough to state that a value judgment is a disguised form of an imperative or a norm; such a statement must be proved. In our judgment this is an erroneous assumption.

If there is any relation between norms and value judgments, such relationship consists, in our opinion, in

1. Cf. *Religion and Science* (New York: Henry Holt, 1935), p. 238.

the fact that the norms, in order to be valid, must be based on the corresponding value judgments. Hence, value research should precede the normative.

As can be seen, the automatic elimination of that which contradicts one's own doctrine, is not a monopoly of rationalism or objectivism. We have already pointed out in a previous section[2] the errors which Ayer commits when he excludes elements which do not coincide with his theory, and admits only that which is favorable. He maintains that values do not add anything to the content of a proposition, and that we never really discuss values but facts.

Value judgments, according to Ayer, do not assert anything; they are the mere expression of the feeling of the speaker; they may also be meant to arouse feeling and so to stimulate action. That is true; but only in some cases. On the other hand, even empirical statements may express an emotion or arouse feeling and stimulate action. If we say "the house is on fire" we make an empirical statement that, at the same time, may express a lot of emotion. And it will evidently arouse some emotion in the hearer and to stimulate him to action: helping to put the fire out or calling the fire department.

To express an emotion is not, therefore a distinctive characteristic of value judgments. Someone may reply that not *all* empirical judgments express an emotion, while value judgments do. But it is not true that all value judgments express emotions. Let us consider an example.

I have a moral conflict and I do not know what to do. I want to do what I *ought* to do, and as I have been concerned with ethics for many years, I want to have reasons for my decision. I want to examine the facts and see if there is any valid moral norm that could be

2. Cf. Chap. III, n. 55.

applicable. Should I behave according to Kant's categorical imperative, or the ten commandments or some other moral norm? If I finally decide in favor of one of the alternatives and say "this is the right thing to do," I am not expressing any emotion, but only an evaluation at the end of an intellectual analysis. There are many other situations of a similar order.

In cases like this, I am not expressing an emotion because there is no emotion to express. The evaluation of alternative ways of behavior—that could be hypothetical possibilities—may be the result of a rational, philosophical and unemotional analysis.

In some cases the moral decision and behavior consist mainly in checking the emotions, in resisting the pressure of drives, inclinations and feelings. The moral will, as in the case of Kant's ethics, could be rationally guided. It could even be the case that my decision is opposed to my emotions as when I help a man, whom I hate, because I think that it is my duty to help him, and I arrive at the conclusion that it is my duty after a rational analysis of the situation, as in Kant's categorical imperative.

The other fundamental statement made by Ayer is that we never discuss values but only facts. This is an empirical statement that should be tested against the facts. Undoubtedly, many of our discussions of ethical and esthetic questions are only discussions about facts. Is it true that our discussions never refer to value? There is not the slightest doubt that many of our disagreements over ethical and esthetic problems are in substance only discussions involving facts; that we frequently differ because there is disagreement over factual elements. Does something similar occur in all cases? We do not think so. There are situations in which the participants are fully in agreement over the facts, but differ for strictly axiological reasons. This is what happens in the case of certain art critics who are in agreement over the facts relating to a painting or a musical composition, yet who, nevertheless, disagree because they have differing conceptions of the nature of esthetic value. Similarly, this occurs when the disagreement does not refer to an isolated value, but to the position which a given value occupies with respect to another value in the axiological table.

Ayer is mistaken in thinking that only people of different cultural or social communities have different axiological tables. One frequently finds basic axiological discrepancies among members of the same family, who live under a common roof and have been educated in the same schools. In one, religious values predominate; in another, economic; and in a third, esthetic. This predominance is, rather, contingent upon psychological types, as Spranger has shown, and not upon educational or circumstantial situations. The discussions in that family refer to values, not to facts, i.e., to the hierarchical order which one value ought to occupy with respect to another.

An argument that carries more weight is the case of deliberation in the same person. The knowledge of facts cannot be different; the alternative has to refer to values.

Ayer arrives at certain conclusions in ethics and esthetics as a result of the application of his epistemological hypothesis, and with the idea—as he expressly states—of giving an account of value judgments "consistent with our general empiricist principles."[3]

Esthetic and moral education does not only consist in calling the young man's attention to certain questions of fact, or consequences produced by certain actions, but also in directing his attention toward values which his inexperienced observations have not as yet discovered.

---

3. *Language, Truth and Logic*, p. 102. In the Introduction he wrote: "I do not deny that in putting forward this theory [emotive theory] I was concerned with maintaining the general consistency of my position." *Ibid.*, p. 20.

Ayer's central thesis, it will be recalled, consists in asserting that value judgments are neither true nor false, since they do not state anything, but evince instead the feelings of the one who makes the judgment. In an examination of this thesis, John Dewey reproaches its author for the ambiguity contained in the words "feelings" and "evince;"[4] this is a serious reproach, especially if one bears in mind that it is directed at a man who focuses the problem in terms of semantic analysis.

Bertrand Russell's thesis, as we have seen, is very similar to Ayer's and consequently lends itself to criticism similar to that stated above. Let us examine separately those aspects of his thesis which do not exactly coincide with Ayer's position.

One of them refers to the leap from the difficulty of finding valid arguments to prove that something has value to the negation of the existence of intrinsic values. Aside from the error of such an inference, one must point out the haste with which Russell affirms the "complete impossiblity" of finding such arguments. If he had abided by the facts, he should have stated that he did not know, up to that moment, of any argument which, in his opinion, would prove the existence of intrinsic values. There can be no "essential" reason which prevents anyone from finding valid arguments in the future; on the other hand, Russell, who is an empiricist, cannot appeal to immutable essences. If scientists had adopted a similar approach in the past, with respect to the existence of bacteria, for example, they still would not have discovered them. The difficulties in noting their presence did not close the door to the possibility of their eventual discovery. Is it not possible perhaps that intense and constant study in the field of

4. Cf. John Dewey, *Theory of Valuation*, International Encyclopedia of Unified Sciences, Vol. II, No. 4 (Chicago: The University of Chicago Press, 1939), pp. 8-12.

axiology may, later on, make it plain that something
actually does have intrinsic value?[5]

When Russell refuses to accept the existence of an
axiological criterion, for lack of proof, he is assuming,
without proving it, of course, the superiority of logical
value over other values. Why should we deny value to that
which cannot be proved logically? Can one prove that
what is proved has greater value than what cannot be
proved?

The contradiction between his statements and his
behavior is common in Russell. For example, he adheres to
the doctrine of the subjectivity of values, and then he
behaves as though values were objective. He writes: "If
two men differ over values, there is no disagreement as to
the kind of truth, but a difference of taste."[6] He adds that
something has value in the degree to which it satisfies a
personal desire. This does not prevent him from advocating
"the cultivation of large and generous desires" and to favor
the "happiness of mankind."[7]

What can a "large and generous" desire consist of, if
value depends exclusively upon desire? Without meaning
to, he notes the inadequacy of the definition of value in
terms of desire, and he has to introduce an axiological
element as an adjective of desire. Value is rooted in the
adjective—and not in the noun. A "small" desire is as much
a desire as a "large" one. It is not the desire, therefore,
which confers value, but the *kind* of desire. If there is no
argument to prove that something is valuable, neither is

5. Russell himself anticipated this criticism in 1910 when he wrote: "But
difficulty in discovering the truth does not prove that there is no truth to be
discovered." "The Elements of Ethics," in *Philosophical Essays*, 1910 ed., p.
10; 1966 ed., p. 20.

6. *Religion and Science* (New York: Henry Holt, 1935), pp. 237-38.

7. *Ibid.*, pp. 242-43.

there any to show that a "large" desire is better than a "small" one. However, the paucity of argument does not prevent him from defending "large," "generous" and "impersonal" desires, and becoming indignant in the face of unjust acts, and his moral attitudes are not arbitrary; he gives reasons to support them.

When he is criticized somewhat along these lines,[8] he replies: "I am accused of inconsistency, perhaps justly, because, although I hold ultimate ethical valuations to the subjective, I nevertheless allow myself emphatic opinions on ethical questions. If there is an inconsistency, it is one that I cannot get rid of without insincerity; moreover, an inconsistent system may well contain less falsehood than a consistent one. . . . I am not prepared to forego my right to feel and express ethical passions; no amount of logic, even though it be my own, will persuade me that I ought to do so. There are some men whom I admire, and others whom I think vile; some political systems seem to me tolerable, others an abomination. Pleasure in the spectacle of cruelty horrifies me, and I am not ashamed of the fact that it does. I am no more prepared to give up all this than I am to give up the multiplication table."[9]

This reply proves the excellent quality of the man behind the thinker and, at the same time, the weakness of the theory. In fact, such a theory must be weak, a theory which forces its author, who has acquired a well-deserved reputation for the quality of his logical contributions, to renounce logical consistency in order to be able to uphold such a theory. The whole contradiction is rooted in the fact that Russell, as a man, is convinced of the existence of

8. See the criticism by Justus Buchler in *The Philosophy of Bertrand Russell*, ed. by P. A. Schilpp (Evanston: Northwestern University, 1944), pp. 513-35. Now published by Open Court, La Salle, Illinois.

9. *Ibid.*, p. 720.

justice, decency and dignity, and this conviction is what makes him rebel against injustice, dishonesty and the debasing pleasure of certain spectacles. If he really believed that justice is a question "of tastes" or of mere personal desires, he would not be able to accuse his neighbor of having "improper" or "petty" desires; he would have to respect the desires and tastes of his neighbor, as the latter is supposed to respect his.

This is the source of the basic weakness and unsatisfactory nature of subjectivism, regardless of whether it proclaims desire, pleasure or interest as the basic notion in the interpretation of value; it actually consists in the fact that it leaves the axiological problem untouched.

In fact, as has already been suggested, if we are to define value in terms of desire, all desire would be valuable. But if it were, we could not speak of "improper," "indecent" or "small" desires, nor of "large," "honest" or "generous" desires. Desire, as desire, is a neutral psychological state brought face to face with values; its ethical quality depends on another element which is necessarily axiological. One must look for a standard outside of desire in order to determine its ethical nature; the same is true for interest and pleasure.

What gives rise to a certain confusion is that desires, pleasures and interests can be good or bad (and, therefore, they are grounded upon ethics) while other psychologic phenomena which exist in the world, cannot be good or bad; they are, consequently, beyond all relationship with values. Thus, our perceptions, our memories, just as triangles and trees, are only good or bad with relation to the behavior—desires and interests—of men.

Whereas it is true that value is given in an actual or possible valuation, it is evident that we must distinguish between valuation, as a psychological fact, and the *validity* of the valuation. If an object acquired value when we value it, there would be no possibility of making a mistake. If everything is true, nothing is true; error gives meaning and force to truth.

It seems to be an undeniable fact that mere positive psychological valuation does not confer a specific value upon an object. The preference of modern youth for "rock music" does not confer upon the latter aesthetic superiority over a sonata by Beethoven. We recognize the superior hierarchy of the sonata over and above individual and collective preferences, and we frequently make use of this superior hierarchy to valuate negatively those individuals who are incapable of taking notice of it. One can tell the difference between a well-educated person from one who lacks education by his interests, desires and preferences.

On the other hand, the desires and actual valuations are not produced capriciously or chaotically; there must be within objective reality some element which forces us to valuate in a certain way. The axiological problem, therefore, does not consist in finding out how or why we valuate, but how we *ought* to valuate. If we want something, it is because we think we recognize in the object the presence of some quality which makes it worthy of our desire. This fact permits us to point out a difference which is basic in axiology, and which was suggested by Ehrenfels at the close of the last century in this polemic with Meinong, and repeated subsequently by several thinkers in different countries: we refer to the distinction between the desired and the desirable.[10]

Any inquiry into what people actually desire belongs to psychology or sociology; only the "desirable" is strictly

---

10. Because of lack of information, each country attributes this distinction to some national authors; the Americans ascribe it to John Dewey. The distinction was made in 1897 by Ch. von Ehrenfels in his *System der Werttheorie*, Vol. I, pp. 53 ff.

axiological. This distinction does not, of course, imply complete separation between the two. The "desirable" retains its umbilical cord which unites it to the "desired." Could anything ever be desirable if no one desired it or could ever desire it? Absolute separation transforms the value of the "desirable" into a mere hollow formula; the identification of the "desirable" with the "desired" opens the door to axiological chaos. Such reduction is typical of the subjectivists.[11] "What we 'ought' to desire," writes Russell, "is merely what someone else wishes us to desire."[12] But there is no way to justify this wish since all desires carry the same weight. Is education possible if one accepts such a theory?

2. The Errors of Axiological Objectivism

The exaggerations of axiological subjectivism which we have indicated have served to reinforce the objectivist thesis. But there is no philosophical school which can be erected on the errors of an opposing doctrine. On the other hand, subjectivism is partly right; its mistake derives from the reduction of the totality to one of its components. The subjectivists have gone so far in repudiating the objectivists that they have erred as far in the opposite direction.

For objectivism, as we have seen, values are independent of value objects and of the subjects who valuate them; moreover, they are absolute and unchangeable, and cannot be affected by any actual

11. For our criticisms on Perry's interpretation of value, see Chap. III, pp. 54-59.

12. *What I Believe*, p. 29.

physical or human event. The nature of the human being, the changes undergone in the course of history, the constant flux of his preferences, the vicissitudes of man's desires and interests—all of these leave values intact and unaffected. "Values are independent of the entire organization of any given spiritual being,"[13] writes Scheler. Farther on, he stresses the point that "just as the existence of objects (e.g., numbers) or nature does not imply an 'ego,' much less so is one implied by the existence of values."[14] And he goes on to reject

> any theory which tries to limit the very essence of value to men and to their make-up whether this be 'psychic' or 'psycho-physical'; that is to say, any theory which attempts to place the essence of value in relation to man or his nature.[15]

Scheler removes value so completely from all relationship with human reality that he imprisons himself within his own definition and places himself, in this way, beyond reach of all criticism. In making use of this procedure, he only succeeds in committing the error of stating something which reality does not confirm, or conversely, remaining in the sterile area of tautology.

He argues, for example, that "even though murder had never been 'judged' to be bad, it would continue being bad. And even though the good had never been 'evaluated' as 'good,' it would nevertheless be good."[16] Why is murder bad if people do not consider it so? Simply because in the definition itself there is implied a negative valuation of murder, i.e., its rejection. Since it had at first

13. M. Scheler, *Der Formalismus*, p. 275.

14. *Ibid.*, p. 280.

15. *Loc. cit.*

16. *Ibid.*, p. 67.

been defined as bad, it must subsequently be considered bad. Substitute the word homicide for murder, and it will be seen that its positive or negative valuation depends on the motives, causes, purposes and situation in which homicide is carried out. That is to say, we have to take these actual facts into account in order to know whether a homicide should be evaluated positively or negatively.

The tautological character of Scheler's statements is seen more clearly in the second example which he offers, and which amounts to maintaining that good is good. Such a statement is as true as it is fruitless. What is of interest is to know what the good consists of. There can be no doubt that in the course of history people have often changed their ideas of what is good. Can we determine the nature of good with complete disregard for what humanity considers it to be?

Scheler and other philosophers who take refuge in the a priori in order, possibly, to avoid being contradicted by reality, are not playing the game according to the rules. From reality they extract concepts which constitute their theories, and then, severing all connections with experience, they transform these concepts, which are of empirical origin, into immutable a priori essences. Since such essences are what they are by definition, there is not the slightest possibility of questioning them. A typical example of this exaggeration, based on a simple tautology, is Scheler's statement that the nutritive is nutritive, although it may be harmful to the health of some people. Those individuals that do not adjust to the definition are "abnormal." Scheler is not interested in the fact that the concept of nutrition is relational and conditional in nature; that one man's meat is another man's poison, and that even so far as the same person is concerned, what saves his life today may kill him tomorrow. Scheler ignores the facts and sticks to his tautological assertion: nutritive is nutritive.

Scheler's ambiguous attitude towards experience becomes evident when one examines his criteria for determining the hierarchy of values.

As will be recalled, Scheler's axiological table is a priori, i.e., it does not depend at all upon the actual reactions which the subjects may experience. "This hierarchy," he writes, "just as the distinction between 'positive' and 'negative' values, resides in the very *essence* of values, and is not only applicable to 'values which are known' by us."[17] The axiological hierarchy, as we have seen, is grasped by means of a special act of cognition, known as preference. "The higher essence of a value is unavoidably and essentially 'given' only in the act of preferring."[18] Although the superiority of a value is not given us before preferring, but only in preferring, this superiority, for Scheler, does not consist in the fact that the value has actually been preferred.

Scheler had to indicate some concrete manner of apprehending the axiological hierarchy in order that his theory not be left completely up in the air. But as he could not base such superiority upon the empirical fact he had to affirm that "only" in preference is the superiority of a value made evident, but that such superiority is not caused by our preferences. If the only method does not assure us of the superiority of one value over another, how can we know what is the case? How can we know that the preference has not been deceptive?

On the other hand, since preference is a concrete psychological act, it will be necessary to determine which types of preference are really indicative of axiological superiority, and in which persons and under what circumstances these acts of preference will occur? It is

17. *Ibid.*, p. 107.

18. *Loc. cit.*

clear that preference varies with age, sex, cultures and from one individual to another. Even in the same person, at different stages or in different circumstances, preferences vary with respect to value objects as well as values. What kind of preference should we prefer? Preferring by itself will not suffice for the determination of the hierarchy of a value: what is required is a qualifier, an indication of an actual standard by which to distinguish the valid preferences from the false ones, since Scheler himself admits—and this time rightly so—that sometimes we prefer low rather than higher values.

This desire, as well as a lack of desire, to rely upon experience, places Scheler in the somewhat embarrassing position of the inept cyclist who, from time to time, has to rest his foot on the ground in order to keep his balance, but who raises it as soon as he succeeds in regaining balance, or someone reproaches him for doing what he should not do.

Similar criticism can be made of Scheler's criteria for determining the axiological hierarchy, particularly the criterion of "the depth of satisfaction." Although the weight of values "does not *consist* in the depth of satisfaction we experience, nevertheless by a connection of essences, the 'higher' value also yields a more profound satisfaction."[19]

How can it be said that the higher value produces a deeper satisfaction through a "connection of essences," when this is quite often not the case? We shall have to repeat once again the questions asked previously: In which persons are we going to "measure" this supposed depth of satisfaction? Under what circumstances?

Scheler's ambiguous attitude is likewise revealed when he proposes duration and divisibility as criteria for the

19. *Ibid.*, p. 116.

determination of his hierarchy. This ambiguity consists in giving consideration to value objects, much less to the value carriers, for otherwise duration would be assured by virtue of the material which has been selected. Then, refers to values. "Superior *values*, not goods, are necessarily and essentially given as lasting."[20] He states farther on that "values which are inferior are also evanescent; superior values are at the same time eternal."[21] What is the meaning of the statement that inferior values are evanescent? Superior values, as values, are just as atemporal as inferior values. Brevity or permanence will have to refer in some way to goods or to experiences which apprehend values. He writes:

> These experiences will always appear as 'lasting' or 'changeable,' to whoever wants it that way, whenever he wants it, and for as long as they may wish to last. When we experience them, without having to await the experience of their *factual duration*, we already experience within their very selves a definitive duration, pertaining to their essence.[22]

How do we know that we experience a "definitive duration" when, as a matter of fact, the exact opposite occurs? He maintains that "it belongs to the *essence* of the authentic act of love to be *sub specie quadam aeterni* . . . and this connection of essences persists—irrespective of the factual duration of actual love—for the actual person in objective time."[23] The adolescent experiences his first amorous passion with a duration that seems eternal to him. Nevertheless, this does not prevent him from changing

20. *Ibid.*, p. 111.

21. *Ibid.*, p. 113.

22. *Ibid.*, p. 112.

23. *Ibid.*, pp. 111-12.

sweethearts in a few months. What is involved here is an illusion, Scheler would probably say, and not an essentially lasting love. How can we be sure not to fall prey to illusions, similar to those of the adolescent? To assert that it belongs to the essence of authentic love to be *sub specie quadam aeterni*, when actual loves are transitory is equivalent to saying what fits one's theory. On the other hand, love experiences are not stable; they are changeable. The love of the elderly couple who celebrate their fiftieth wedding anniversary is quite different from the love they have experienced as courting sweethearts. It is a different *type* of experience.

Scheler seeks to check the flux and movement of the world, and since he encounters resistance, he transforms actual realities into essences by magic, with the resultant advantage, for him, that essences are more docile than realities. It is enough to define them in a certain way in order that they continue behaving that way without danger of contradiction. The trouble is that many eternal essences have gone with the wind, after conceptual and terminological clarification or scientific advance. It is true that in the world of essences, one is protected from facts; the trouble is that one will eventually be rudely awakened by reality.

A similar play between values and value objects results from the proposal to consider divisibility as a criterion for hierarchy. He writes: "Values are doubtless 'higher' to the extent that they are less 'divisible,' i.e., the less they have to be 'split up' by the *many that partake of them*."[24] Values, because they are unspatial essences, lack the possibility of being divided, and the participation of many people in so-called "divisible" values is similar to that which can exist in the highest values: we can all partake

24. *Ibid.*, p. 113.

equally in pleasure as well as in esthetic enjoyment. What happens is that in order to enjoy the pleasure of a meal, for example, we have to consume it, whereas we can enjoy a painting without altering it. But this may be the case of low values as well: the pleasure derived from swimming in the ocean or from spring temperature does not need either division or consumption.

As for goods, all are more or less divisible, and the nature of the divisibility depends largely upon the corresponding carrier. In a store it is probably true that "a piece of cloth is worth approximately twice that of half of the cloth;"[25] however, circumstances may confer upon that half a higher value than what the whole was worth originally, if e.g., there is a shortage of the material, necessary for finishing the garment, or else, that half may come down in value, which is what happens if there is a surplus of cloth.

Of all the criteria proposed by Scheler, the most consistent is the one called "foundation." This is undoubtedly because a rational element is to be found here. The basic value must occupy a higher position in the hierarchy than the value which is based upon it, since the latter exists as a function of the former. For this reason, an intrinsic value is superior to the corresponding instrumental value, since the latter derives its value from the fact that it is a means to achieve the intrinsic value.

Even when he propounds this criterion, Scheler still makes statements which do not seem to correspond to reality. He maintains, for example, that "the pleasure value—I refer to the pleasant as a value—according to the laws of essences, is 'based' upon a vital value: e.g., health."[26] It would seem, in fact, that things which please

25. *Loc. cit.*

26. *Ibid.*, p. 115.

us, strengthen our health, and that those which call forth
our distaste can harm it. Of course, it is not always so;
children are well aware of this fact.

Since facts appear to contradict his thesis, Scheler is
forced to shift his statement concerning facts to the level
of essences. He writes that

> this principle, like the law of essences, is completely
> independent of *inductive* experiences which men have, e.g.,
> concerning the relationship between factual health and
> sickness, and feelings of pleasure and displeasure, such as, for
> instance, the following facts: that many lung diseases, death
> by asphyxia at a certain stage, and euphoria in paralysis, are
> linked with strong feelings of pleasure.[27]

And in order to prove what he asserts, he asks himself:
"Who, no matter how unfortunate he may be, 'would
envy' the paralytic because of his euphoria?"[28] Perhaps
few would envy the paralytic, but there are many who
envy those who take narcotics and other harmful and
pleasant drugs. As usual, the empirical proof carries little
weight.

"Foundation," in Scheler, has a theological basis. He
wants to arrange all values, starting with the one which is
highest. He says so expressly: "All possible values are
based *(fundiert)* upon *the value of a personal and infinite
Spirit* and on a *'universe of values'* which stems
therefrom."[29] This position assumes the denial of the
autonomy of the different axiological areas, which is one
of the achievements of modern thought. Although values
maintain relationships among themselves, the areas of

27. *Loc. cit.*

28. *Loc. cit.*

29. *Ibid.*, p. 116.

esthetic, ethical and religious values are individually autonomous. Scheler does away with this autonomy in setting up his table in accord with the regulating principle of religious values, which recalls the medieval attitude. On the other hand, to base axiology on theological dogma is to establish it on a rather weak foundation: the change which Scheler underwent proves this clearly. What did Scheler think of this entire hierarchical order, based on "the law of essences" and founded on a personal and infinite Spirit, when he broke with that theological conception? This break was life's retort to the vain pretension of wishing to erect something forever upon the shaky foundations of a supposed a priori knowledge.[30]

3. Overcoming the Antithesis

Let it not be thought for one moment that all of Scheler's work has been in vain. Insofar as his eidetic statements are based on real facts, he has left us with analyses and insights which ought definitely to be incorporated into the development of axiology. Where he errs is in the exaggeration of his point of view, just as is the case with the subjectivists.

The original error in both schools of thought is to be found in the fallacy of false opposition. Since each school believes that value necessarily has to be either objective or subjective, each clings blindly to its own thesis, as it takes note of the errors of its opponent. Russell's argument in favor of subjectivism, it will be recalled, rests on a lack of convincing proof of the objectivist thesis. The moral and

---

30. For a short statement of his new theological doctrine, see our quotation on pp. 92-93.

educational consequences which flow from the subjectivist position have, in turn, served to bolster objectivism, albeit artificially so.

If we wish to abide by the nature of values rather than the coherence of our own theory, we should rephrase the question. Do values necessarily have to be objective or subjective? Are all values of a similar nature? What should be the point of departure in our study, if we are to adhere closely to reality and not to our own creations?

In trying to answer the first question, we should perhaps take note of the fact that the psychological experiences of pleasure, desire and interest are a necessary, but not a sufficient, condition; on the other hand, these experiences do not exclude objective elements, but rather assume them. If this were so, value would be the result of a relationship or tension between subject and object, and would have a subjective as well as an objective side.

If, in the course of our inquiry, we were to note that this is so, it would then be our task to find out if the proportion of the two integrating elements can be applied to all values. It might well be that the axiological scale would be determined exactly by the progressive increase of one of these two elements.

The third question is the most important one at this time in which an *impasse* seems to have been reached in the axiological problem. What is the reality from which we should take our point of departure?

A philosophy which postulates certain entities and which then adheres to its own definitions may attain a maximum of coherence, but it will never succeed in offering an explanation of actual reality. Philosophic theory should be measured by the coherence of its conceptual scheme, as well as, at the same time, by the capacity it possesses for explaining the facts of this world. In studying Scheler's theory, we see his logical coherence and his capacity for calling forth emotional attachment;

nevertheless, we reproach him for his lack of consideration of real experience.

Even Scheler recognizes the fact that philosophy, and particularly ethics, should start with experience. He writes: "Knowledge, regardless of its nature, is rooted in experience. Ethics, also, in turn, should be based on 'experience'."[31] This does not prevent him from subsequently sailing amidst clouds of essences.

Verbal adherence to experience by a theory is not enough to make it empirical. It is necessary to determine clearly what is meant by experience, and not to ignore it when experience contradicts our views.

On a previous occasion we examined the concept of experience and showed in what way it is the necessary point of departure and permanent reference of all genuine philosophizing.[32] Upon again considering the problem vis-à-vis the axiological question, we note that the interpretative outline of experience maintains its validity. Here, too, there is, in fact, an activity and an object of such activity. The object is the value which appears evident to the intentional consciousness which valuates.

When dealing with values, one must be careful not to fall into an error similar to that which has been made many times when discussing the nature of physical objects and the knowledge we have of them. Many have asked themselves if the sound of an object falling in an uninhabited desert really "exists." The two antithetical interpretations seem equally valid, because there is ambiguity in the statement of the problem, and each one considers a different aspect of the question. The sound, as sound, does not exist, of course, if there is no ear to hear

---

31. Cf. *op. cit.*, p. 179.

32. Cf. Risieri Frondizi, *El punto de partida del filosofar* (2d ed.; Buenos Aires: Edit. Losada, 1957), Chapters III and IV.

it; a sound is a sound which is heard. If, on the other hand, one understands the existence of the sound to be the vibrations which the object produces upon falling, the situation is quite different, since such existence does not require the presence of a sense of hearing. In the analysis of gustatory perceptions, the distinction turn out to be very evident. If we understand by "sweet" the corresponding experience of gustatory perception, this cannot exist without a palate, i.e., without a subject that has the experience; sugar is not sweet when it is inside a container. On the other hand, if we understand by the term "sweet" the physico-chemical properties contained in sugar, and which can produce in us the gustatory perception of "sweet," such properties are independent of the subject that can taste the sugar.

If we examine the relationship between the valuable object and the subject that valuates it, we will notice clearly, once the ambiguity vanishes, that the value can exist only in relation to a subject that valuates it. What meaning would the enjoyment of a meal have without a palate capable of "converting" the physico-chemical properties of the meal into a pleasurable experience? We usually say the "meal" is pleasant because we refer the experience to what causes it. The same is true with esthetic values, i.e., musical or pictorial, which exist only in relation to subjects with auditory and visual sensitivity.

Besides the subject and object, one must take into consideration the "activity" of the subject, by means of which the latter places himself in relation to the object; in the case of values, this activity is the process of valuation. A subject valuating an object will be the point of departure of the analysis. No matter how deep one may go in the analysis, there is no possibility of disconnecting the object from the subject, as the objectivists want, or of reducing everything to the mere subjective experience. The analysis may prove that value is a relational notion requiring both the presence of the subject and the object.

4. Value and Situation

Let us begin by examining a simple case: the pleasure which I feel when I drink a glass of beer. For a subjectivist, all the value of the beer depends on the pleasure which I experience when I drink it; if for any reason, either physiological or psychological, I fail to feel any pleasure, beer is valueless. The objectivist, on the contrary, will insist that the quality is inherent in the beer, and if this were not so, the beer would not afford any pleasure.

As we have seen, pleasure implies the presence of a palate capable of converting the physico-chemical properties of the object into an enjoyable experience; and up to this point, the subjectivist is right. But this is a question of "converting" certain properties found in the object, and not one of creating them. The presence of the object is therefore indispensable in order that valuation may take place.

Yet the above will not suffice. The problem is much more complex, because neither the subject nor the object is homogeneous, or stable. Let us begin with the subject.

I do not always valuate the beer in the same way. The biological and psychological conditions in which I find myself modify my judgment. Thus, for example, if I am thirsty, the beer will produce a different feeling from the one I have after having drunk a good deal of liquid; when I am angry, it has a different flavor from when I am pleased. All the other physiological and psychological conditions are equally influential; from arterial pressure to the attitude which I have toward life, and to my feelings of fatigue, worry or hope, as these affect the functioning of the nervous and glandular system.

The object is also complex. We speak of beer as though it existed as some kind of unchangeable essence, but this is not so. There are different kinds of beer, to judge by their physico-chemical composition. If density, temperature, etc., are changed, the pleasurable feeling will vary. Other objective elements similarly exert an influence: the glass from which one drinks, the temperature of the physical environment in which one finds oneself, etc.

Besides the subjective and objective elements, there are also social and cultural factors which play their part: to have a glass of beer with a friend is not the same as drinking with an enemy: to drink with someone is different from drinking alone. Similarly, to drink in one's own country as opposed to drinking abroad, or in an elegant cocktail lounge as opposed to having one's foot on the rail in a pub, and in questionable company,—all of these are far from identical situations. The tastes we have developed, the prestige of the particular drink—these and a host of other cultural and social elements which constitute the history of the society and culture in which we live, influence the valuation which we make of a simple glass of beer.

We have started out with a simple example in order to see clearly the part played by different elements. If we now pass over from the superficial plane of pleasure to the deeper levels of ethical and esthetic valuation, we will note the increase in complexity and the variants in the proportion of the ingredients. Let us, for example, examine an ethical value. The development of the sociological interpretation of ethics, beginning with the teaching of Durkheim and Lévy-Bruhl, the axiological contributions of Müller-Freienfels and Heyde, have demonstrated the connection which exists between ethical valuation and the actual behavior of men, due to customs, religion, etc., and the legal, economic and social organization of the community in which they live.

Let us take as an example the ethical value upon which the seventh commandment is based. The misconduct which theft implies has meaning only in a society having an economic organization which guarantees private property. What meaning could theft have where property was communal? When the economic system is changed, the value which gives support to the seventh commandment also changes.

In other cases, the character of value is changed for individual reasons. The eighth commandment orders us not to bear false witness. Is this principle valid for a four-year old child? Child psychology reveals to us the world of fantasy in which the child lives, and forces us to treat him on different terms from those we use when we judge adults.

If we take a look at any of the tables of values, upheld by the objectivist axiologists, we will see that they have all been worked out with the adult European man in mind. These tables are the result of the historical evolution of Western culture; if the development had been different—history does not have a fixed course—the table of values would also be different. The development of Christianity, as well as of the Catholic Church as an institution, has influenced the axiological tables and the absolute conceptions of value.

The economic and legal organization, customs, tradition, religious beliefs, and many other forms of life which transcend ethics, have contributed to the shaping of certain moral values, which are then said to exist in a world foreign to the life of man. Although value may not be derived exclusively from factual elements, neither can it be divorced entirely from reality. If we arbitrarily separate values from actual experiences, we are condemned to the bloodless realm of essences.

Nevertheless, let it not be supposed that ethical, esthetic or legal judgments can *be reduced* to the complex of subjective cultural and social circumstances. These circumstances are part, but not all, of the valuation, as we have already indicated: the strictly objective aspect is missing. What would we think of a priest, a judge, or a member of a jury, who would evaluate a man's behavior or an esthetic creation, in accordance with the functioning of his liver, or tradition, or the beliefs and inclinations of the group to which he belongs? In these cases, we require that the object itself be borne in mind—the behavior or the painting—without interference by circumstances which exert pressure upon the subject to evaluate one way or the other. To be a good judge means to be able to resist personal inclinations and preferences and decide "objectively."

The importance of the objective aspect is greater in the ethical or esthetic plane than in that of pleasure, because as one ascends the scale of values, the objective element increases. Whereas our physiological and psychological conditions—thirst, fatigue, anger—are important in the realm of pleasure, they have to surrender their predominance to objective factors in the ethical plane. The weight of the value could therefore be measured by the greater or lesser degree of objectivity.

Whatever is the case under examination or the position of the value in the scale, we shall always be faced with two aspects of the question: subjective and objective.

The movies, as a simple illustration of perception of apparent movement, reveal the joint participation of the objective and subjective factors. As is well known, static pictures are projected onto the screen. If such images are released in quick enough succession, we do not see static but moving pictures. A person who does not know the mechanism of the perception of apparent movement, will find it difficult to admit that the rapid "movements" of a ballerina or the hoof-beats of a race horse that he can clearly "see" on the screen, are not there but in his mind. On the other hand, someone who is aware of the spectator's contribution might commit the error of axiological subjectivism and maintain that all we see is merely a projection of ourselves. The truth is that the spectator's contribution is what permits us to see the object *in motion*, but if there were no static images projected upon the screen, there would be no perception of any sort. The perception in the movies is the synthesis of two factors: the static pictures constitute the objective aspect and the movement is added by the subject. Something similar occurs in the case of values where, without the contribution of the two factors, there would be neither value nor experience of value. In this sense, value is a relational notion, like marriage, for instance.

The relation is neither simple nor static, but complex and changing. It is complex in two senses: (a) because the two factors of the relation are neither homogenous nor simple; (b) the interrelation as such is complex. It should be also pointed out that both the factors and their relation are dynamic.

Let us begin with the subjective aspect. We have already seen that a value has no existence or meaning without a real or possible valuation. The valuation, in turn, changes according to the physiological and psychological conditions of the subject. The nervous system, the functioning of the glands which control internal secretion, arterial pressure, and other aspects of our biological life condition our valuation, especially in those areas which are lowest in the axiological scale.

The dynamic quality of the subjective factor increases in passing from the physiological to the psychological aspects. The valuating experience receives the influence of all the other previous or simultaneous experiences. The way in which visual or auditory cognition takes place influences the valuation of the painting or the musical selection to which we are listening. There is also the influence of the painting we have seen previously, or the selection we listened to a few moments earlier; in fact, all the experiences which have preceded the valuation. The influence of the simultaneous experiences is even greater. A disagreeable odor, a sharp noise, pain, or worry, interfere with the valuation of a painting. The chain of association of ideas which the sight of the painting sets in motion contributes even more to valuation. If we cannot ignore the entire structure of our psychic life at the moment of valuation, how can we fail to take it into account when we examine this problem?

We have adopted a somewhat arbitrary procedure when speaking of simultaneous experiences subjected to valuation. Neither the evaluating experience nor the experiences which accompany it are fixed; instead, they are in flux and maintain a mutual relationship to one another. The intensity of an esthetic feeling can deaden or diminish the pain or worry which was present at the moment of viewing the painting. This fluctuation of the valuating experience and of its connections with the other experiences that follow it shows only one side of the complexity pertaining to the subjective factor of valuation. This complexity increases if we take a look at past experiences which appear to continue to operate in the present.

Let us begin with experiences subject to the same type of valuation which we have been considering. In the valuation of a painting, there is present all of our esthetic experience, both positive and negative. The earlier views of the same painting, the paintings by the same artist which we have seen previously, all the painting which we have ever seen in our entire life, together with all the theories of esthetics with which we may be familiar, or which we have arrived at through our own efforts,—all of this is present when we evaluate a single painting. However, since esthetic life cannot be separated from other forms of human life (religious, intellectual, political, etc.) our whole past constitutes the background of every single esthetic experience.

The nature of the objective factor is just as complex. We said that there is no value without valuation; we can now state that there is no valuation without value; valuation requires the presence of an intentional object. There are qualities in the object which make me react in a definite way, to evaluate it positively, although I may not like or wish to do so; which demand my interest, although I might prefer to ignore it, or which do not succeed in awakening my interest, although I might very much want to be interested. It is these objective qualities which give the great works of art their lasting value, in contrast to those works which succeed only in awakening a passing interest.

The aggregate of objective qualities of a painting, capable of arousing a definite emotion within me, does not appear in isolated form: the painting has a frame, it is hung on a wall which is part of a building. The size, color and form of the frame, just as the color and size of the wall, the position of the painting in the room, etc., constitute part of the objective qualities. We can, therefore, increase or reduce the value of a painting by changing the objective conditions which surround it. Among these conditions, besides those already pointed out, light is of primary importance; this does not mean that other physical conditions should be minimized.

The tendency toward abstraction which axiological objectivism has shown, has forced it to speak of values without considering their carriers, as if we had a direct relationship with the former, regardless of specific value objects. The truth is that the values which we know are embodied in objects, and therefore imply a carrier. The relationship between the value and its carrier is more important than it is usually considered to be. If the Chartres Cathedral had been built of bricks, it would have lost a good deal of its esthetic value. One cannot transfer the form of a statue, e.g., from marble to bronze, without altering it; the nature of the material used, its physical resistance, its color and aspect, affect the beauty of the statue. What we say about the statue can be applied to the rest of the esthetic areas and also to the other realms of value.

On the other hand, every value is related to other values. The beauty of a Gothic cathedral cannot be separated from the religious value which inspired it; the esthetic quality of a piece of furniture is not independent of its utility; nor is the justice of a sentence something apart from its consequences.

The relationship between subject and object, in turn, takes place within a given society, culture and historical period. Anyone who has been to a museum or a concert hall, knows the extent to which esthetic feeling depends upon the company present; the very presence, not to mention a foolish or presumptuous remark by certain individuals, may prevent us from fully enjoying a piece of music. This influence is greater or lesser, depending upon the psychological type of the person who experiences it and the nature of those in whose presence he finds himself. There are those who always react as members of a definite group; no one is capable of ridding himself completely of social influence. This statement does not only possess validity in the esthetic plane; it can also be applied to all the other areas, from the pleasurable to the ethical. The value table of the social group to which we belong pressures us as we judge someone's behavior, appreciate a work of art, or enjoy a meal. And, inasmuch as the community in which we live extends outward from the family to the cultures which are most ample in scope, our

valuations are the result of a simultaneous pressure by our
contemporaries, as well as by the creators of ancient
cultures which have been incorporated into our own.

All the essential circumstances of our personality are
present in any of our valuations. At times, we judge as
New Yorkers, at others, as Americans or men of Western
culture. We shed our most intimate personality in social
situations; we are members of a community and we act as
such. And those elements which seem peculiar to our
community quite often stem from other cultural forms
and historical settings.

Besides all the historical and cultural circumstances,
there is the human circumstance to consider: we are men
and we evaluate as human beings. To ask what values
would be like if there were no men is as meaningless as
asking how an object looks when nobody is looking at it.
Any answer which may be offered commits the error of
eliminating and, at the same time, implying the presence of
the observer. We thus evaluate as individuals, as members
of a community, or a given culture or historical period,
and finally, as human beings.

There will always be those who insist on defending the
objectivity and independence of value, and who assert that
the circumstances indicated above serve only to influence
the "apprehension" of value, but not its essence, existence
or meaning. It will be said that value is what it is and our
changing subjective conditions cannot alter it; these can
only modify our capacity for grasping it. Furthermore, it
will be asked: does not a similar phenomenon occur in the
field of mathematics? Our education, capacity and
intelligence influence the apprehension of a mathematical
relationship; nevertheless, the argument goes, the
relationship itself is kept intact, even though our reasoning
may err.

The force of conviction behind this type of reasoning is
based on the analogy with mathematics. The analogy

assumes that values behave like mathematical entities, but no convincing proof has been offered. We know of many theories that state that value is an essence or an ideal object, or behaves as such; we do not know of any that have demonstrated this or that have offered valid arguments in support of this thesis.

The supposed proofs in favor of the objectivity and independence of value are based, as in Scheler, on the more treacherous forms of subjectivity: the famous emotional intuition. We have already mentioned our justified suspicion of this method of apprehending values, since the values as well as the axiological table, which intuition reveals as objective and absolute, coincide remarkably with the values and table appropriate to the cultural background of the person who possesses this extraordinary intuition.

The coincidence is suspicious and our suspicion increases when the emotional intuition is adjusted to the theory of the person who claims to hold to it, in such a way that the intuitive datum changes when the philosophical theory undergoes a modification. A clear case which illustrates the adjustment of the intuition to the theory, and not vice-versa, is to be found precisely in the greatest supporter of emotional intuition as a form of apprehending values. When Max Scheler breaks with the concept of a personal infinite and perfect God, the infallible intuition which had bestowed such absolute knowledge upon him is adjusted to his new theological conception.

What is to be done in the face of this lack of agreement of supposed infallible intuition within the same person, as in Scheler, or in different persons, as is commonly the case? The intuitive datum cannot be taken as decisive, because one would not know whom to listen to. However, because of these difficulties, one should not err in the opposite direction and completely reject the intuitive datum. Do we lay aside the data, yielded by perception, just because our senses frequently deceive us? The intuitive datum should be gathered up together with other data which human experience affords us. Only the contrast between the various data and the analysis of the different situations in which they are produced, will allow us an interpretation of a complete and integral experience.

When absolute realism tries to escape from the slippery ground of emotional intuition, it lands in the barren field of tautology. As will be recalled, Scheler maintains that, although murder might never have been judged to be bad, it would be so, nevertheless, and that even though the good might never have been evaluated as good, it would still be good. The statement, good is good, is as true as it is barren; the evil inherent in murder is implicit in the definition. When we descend from the level of abstractions to that of reality, formal definitions are of little use. If the nutritive is nutritive, as Scheler states, although it may kill us, we would not know how to conduct ourselves in presence of something which is nutritive by definition and fatal by experience. The same is true in the case of the pleasant which will have to be pleasant although it may disgust us, and is so without regard to the physiological and psychological habits and conditions of the person who evaluates. On the other hand, since we cannot rid ourselves of such habits, what physiological and psychological conditions are necessary in order to apprehend the "objective" pleasure of something which is pleasant by definition? It seems obvious that no one—although he may claim to possess the rare ability of grasping essences in thin air—is capable of divorcing himself from physiological and psychological conditions and other personal and social circumstances.

The importance of such circumstances is seen when one considers those cases in which the presence of value depends on facts and concrete situations. For example, a food which is nutritive for a certain individual is not so for another; the drug which saves a man can kill his wife, or the man himself if the circumstances vary. We usually express ourselves in general terms because we assume common circumstances. We say milk is nutritive because it is so for the majority of people; for certain other people, it is more harmful than alcohol. To assert that milk is nutritive "in itself" is meaningless, since this quality changes as the conditions of the subject who drinks it undergo variation.

An example taken from the esthetic realm will perhaps show up more clearly the dependence of value upon circumstances. Is a lady's elegant-looking hat elegant? Evidently so, by definition. Its owner displays it proudly and excites the admiration of all who are present. What happens if we introduce some change in the clothes of the lady who wears it? If we take her shoes off, for example, or if we replace the dress which matches her hat with a bathing suit? It is obvious that the elegance of the hat is diminished, since it cannot be isolated from the rest of the garments which go with it. Nor can it be separated from the milieu, the style, the social prestige of the person who wears it, the accepted customs, the age, and other personal and social factors. Hence, the woman's elegant hat looks ridiculous on her husband's head, or if she wears it while washing dishes.

More complex examples in the esthetic or ethical realm can reveal better the dependence of value on a host of factors, transitory and permanent, individual and social, which intervene in the valuation of an object.

If the name "situation" is applied to the complex of individual, social, cultural and historical elements and circumstances, then we maintain that values have existence and meaning only within a specific situation.

5. Value as a Gestalt Quality

Even if we isolate value from a given situation, its nature is still very complex. The complexity arises in part from the relation between the value and its empirical qualities. There are philosophers who try to reduce value to its empirical qualities, either the subjective qualities of pleasure, interest or desire or the objective primary and secondary qualities. Other philosophers, on discovering that at times the empirical or natural qualities are present and yet the object lacks value, like G. E. Moore, isolate value from the natural qualities and claim that it is undefinable because it is a simple quality like "yellow."

I think that Moore is right when he points out the difficulties of defining value, but wrong when he assumes that those difficulties are due to the fact that value is a simple quality. I believe exactly the opposite, that value is very complex, and that is why it is really difficult to define. It is a Gestalt quality (*Gestaltqualität*).

The difficulty springs from an "either-or" way of thinking, that value has to be an empirical, natural quality, *or* that it has nothing to do with empirical qualities and is a nonnatural quality grasped by intuition. If it is a simple empirical quality we may apprehend it through one of the senses; and if it is a complex empirical quality, it should be able to be broken down into the simple qualities of which it is composed. This way of reasoning, common among English-speaking philosophers, implies a reduction of empiricism to the atomistic variety. Atomism, of the Humean type, is the basis of the analytic attitude.

If we start from this atomistic assumption, we are condemned to not seeing the qualities that spring from the configuration of the parts. It seems clear that value cannot be reduced to its empirical qualities since once we know all the empirical qualities of a painting or a statue, for instance, we still may ask whether it is beautiful. If beauty could be reduced to its empirical qualities and is defined by those qualities, the question would be meaningless, since it would be equivalent to asking if what is beautiful is beautiful. On the other hand, if we define value as a subjective natural quality, such as pleasure, desire or interest, we still have the open question: Is pleasure, after all, good? Is what I desire "desirable"? These are legitimate questions that would be meaningless if values are reduced to the natural qualities.

Values seem to have an antithetical nature. They cannot be *separated* from the empirical qualities and yet neither can they be *reduced* to them. I believe this is the case because value is a Gestalt quality.

A Gestalt is not equivalent to the sum of its parts, though it cannot exist without them. It is not a metaphysical notion but a concrete, singular entity.

The parts or members of a Gestalt are not homogenous, and here lies the difference between a Gestalt and a mere sum of parts. A quart of water or milk is made up of two pints which can be separated without altering its nature. But we cannot cut a person in two and have two equal living parts. On the moral level, this is more evident: an honest person is neither equivalent to two half-persons who are honest, nor to two persons who are half-honest. A Gestalt, like an honest person, is indivisible. In the case of water, the physical and chemical properties of each drop are similar to the whole; but this is not so in the case of a Gestalt. A symphony orchestra—a typical instance of an organic whole or Gestalt—is made up of different types of individuals who play different instruments. The quality of the orchestra is not equal to the sum of its musicians. Some can be replaced and the unity of the orchestra will still be kept. Each musician plays his part, and the role of the conductor is to give a structural unity to the diversity of instruments.[33]

Another good elementary instance of an axiological Gestalt could be an Ikebana flower arrangement. Even more important than the flowers is the way they are arranged. When we see what an expert can do with the same flowers used by a novice, we easily realize that the beauty of the whole depends more on the interrelation of the flowers than on the intrinsic quality of each one of them. It is true that you cannot have a bouquet or an Ikebana arrangement without flowers but it is no less true that the beauty of the arrangement cannot be found in the mere aggregate of the flowers, nor in any of the individual flowers. When the flowers are scattered on a table, they lack the esthetic appearance of the bouquet.[34]

If we move from the bouquet to a particular flower, we see that the beauty is a Gestalt quality that springs from its shape, color, size, perfume and other sensible qualities; but again it is the totality and not the mere aggregates of such qualities which accounts for the beauty of the flower. We can change some of the sensible qualities—the color, for instance—without breaking the esthetic pattern. But we cannot take all the qualities away and still keep the beauty of it.

The esthetic structure is not an abstraction nor a concept; it is a unity that we find in everyday experience. There is an internal interrelation in the Gestalt, and that is why, when a member is changed it may affect all the other

33. For a criticism of the notion of Gestalt, as it is used here, see Ernest Nagel, "Wholes, Sums, and Organic Unities," in D. Lerner (ed.), *Parts and Wholes* (New York: The Free Press of Glencoe, 1963), pp. 135-55.

34. Even B. Russell who has an analytic mind and attitude admitted the existence of organic wholes. He wrote in 1931: "I am not the least anxious to deny that wholes have important properties not necessarily deducible from their constituents and the relations among these." Charles W. Morris, *Six Theories of Mind* (Chicago: University of Chicago Press, 1932), p. 137.

members. We should not be surprised that the Gestalt quality of the bouquet is made up of flowers which are also Gestalts. This is the usual case. The second act in *Hamlet*, which is an esthetic Gestalt, is part of a larger Gestalt that is *Hamlet*, which at the same time is a part of a larger Gestalt, namely, Shakespeare's theatre.

It is easy to see that the esthetic Gestalt depends upon empirical, sensible qualities. If Miss America gains 100 pounds, her beauty is gone, because the interrelation of several proportions is broken. On the other hand, we can change the color of her skin without affecting her beauty.

The best illustration that the esthetic Gestalt cannot be reduced to the mere aggregate of its members is the case of the transposition of a melody. When we transpose a melody all the sounds of which it is made are different and yet, the melody remains the same.

The analytic approach to value was inadequate because it misses the structural quality. Finally, it led to the naturalistic fallacy pointed out by G. E. Moore. But unfortunately, when he confronted the difficulty, he headed for the dead end of intuitionism. The apparently antithetical nature of value could not make sense for him, namely, that the good was not a natural quality and, at the same time, depended on natural qualities. He wrote:

> Indeed it seems to me to be one of the most important truths about predicates of value, that though many of them *are* intrinsic kinds of value, in the sense I have defined, yet *none* of them are intrinsic properties, in the sense in which such properties as ''yellow'' . . . are intrinsic properties . . . Two different propositions are both true of *goodness*, namely: (1) that it does depend *only* on the intrinsic nature of what possesses it . . . and (2) that, *though* this is so, it is yet not itself an intrinsic property . . . It was for this reason that I said above that, if there are any intrinsic kinds of value, they would constitute a class of predicates which is, perhaps, unique; for I cannot think of any other predicate which resembles them in respect

of the fact, that though *not* itself intrinsic, yet shares with intrinsic properties the characteristics of depending solely on the intrinsic nature of what possesses it.[35]

The perplexity vanishes if one interprets value as a Gestalt quality, since a Gestalt both depends on its members and cannot be reduced to its members.

The notion of *structure* and *structuralism* are in fashion in France and many other countries.[36] But, unfortunately, it is ambiguous as well as fashionable. We use the words *structure, totality, organic unity* and *wholes* as translation for *Gestalt.* [37]

Let us summarize briefly what we understand by Gestalt. In the first place, a Gestalt has qualities that are not to be found in any of its members nor in the mere sum of all of them, as we have already pointed out. There is novelty in the Gestalt quality. That is why it should not be confused with the mere sums of its parts nor taken as a mechanic aggregate. The totality is what counts and a Gestalt emphasizes the unity of the multiplicity.

The second characteristic of the Gestalt is its concrete, real existence. It has no connection with any meta-empirical entity. It should not be confused with a concept, which is abstract, or with a model which is a simplification of reality. *Gestalt* has been erroneously translated in many languages as *form*. Since Aristotle, *form* is opposed to matter or content; a form without a content

---

35. G. E. Moore, "The Conception of Intrinsic Value," *Philosophical Studies* (London: Routledge & Kegan Paul, 1958), pp. 272-73.

36. *Les Temps Modernes* devoted an entire issue (November, 1966) to *Les Problemes du Structuralisme* and C. Lévi-Strauss's *Anthropologie Structurale* (Paris, 1958) is now famous all over the world. See Chapters XV and XVI.

37. On the notion of *Gestalt* see our book *The Nature of the Self* (New Haven: Yale University Press, 1953), especially pp. 163-74.

is an abstraction. A Gestalt is both the form and the content.

A Gestalt implies, in the third place, totality and interdependence of its members. The interrelation should not be interpreted as a one to one relation, but as an active interrelation that is conditioned by the whole. What counts is the relation of the members within the meaning of the total unity. That is why a Gestalt cannot be broken down without being destroyed, and any analysis should keep the structural unity in mind.

It is a fourth characteristic of the Gestalt that its members are not homogenous. Each member has a different nature and role.

In his critical examination of our situational axiology, Professor Robert S. Hartman pointed out a contradiction between two aspects that we claimed are fundamental, namely, the *irreality* of values and the *real* situation in which they are given to us.[38] But there is no contradiction here, since the irreality of value should be interpreted as a Gestalt quality, which depends on real, empirical qualities. On the other hand, values are embodied in real objects, and as such, they are part of any human experience. All the time we are surrounded by value objects, such as the typewriter I am using, the paper I am writing on, the table, the room, the house and so on.

In brief, value is a Gestalt quality, the synthesis of objective and subjective contribution, and which exists and has meaning only in concrete human situations. It has a double connection with reality since the value structure springs from empirical qualities, and the object in which it is embodied is part of the reality we live in. But, on the other hand, values cannot be reduced to the empirical qualities that support them, nor to the value objects in

38. Robert S. Hartman, *El conocimiento del bien* (Mexico: Fondo de Cultura Economica, 1965), pp. 348-52.

which they are embodied. The possibility of new value objects is always open.

Not only values but also their relations and their hierarchy depend on a concrete situation. We can find two mistakes in the traditional way of conceiving the hierarchy. The first mistake is to believe that it is fixed, unchangeable and valid apart from any situation. The second is to believe that the hierarchy is lineal and vertical, like the rank in the army.

The hierarchy, in our opinion, is the result of a very complex interrelation of values. Such interrelation varies according to the situation of the subject, his needs and possibilities, his relation to the object and the situation of the community in which he lives. That is why it is always situational, and has no meaning in the vacuum. Besides, the ever-enriching axiological development of mankind depends upon, and is furthered by the constant exercise of man's imagination, intelligence and action.

Index

DATE DUE

FEB 1 2 1978			
APR 1 3 1978			
3/7/81			
FEB 2 4 1981			
NOV 1 9 1984			
APR 1 1 '88			
OCT 15 '89			
NOV 0 8			
GAYLORD			PRINTED IN U.S.A